TRUTH, LOVE, LIGHT, and SALT

TRUTH, LOVE, LIGHT, and SALT

A Poetic Tribute

SANTOS J. HERNANDEZ JR.

RESOURCE *Publications* • Eugene, Oregon

TRUTH, LOVE, LIGHT, AND SALT
A Poetic Tribute

Copyright © 2021 Santos J. Hernandez Jr. All rights reserved. Except for brief quotations in critical publications or reviews, no part of this book may be reproduced in any manner without prior written permission from the publisher. Write: Permissions, Wipf and Stock Publishers, 199 W. 8th Ave., Suite 3, Eugene, OR 97401.

Resource Publications
An Imprint of Wipf and Stock Publishers
199 W. 8th Ave., Suite 3
Eugene, OR 97401

www.wipfandstock.com

PAPERBACK ISBN: 978-1-6667-0940-7
HARDCOVER ISBN: 978-1-6667-0941-4
EBOOK ISBN: 978-1-6667-0942-1

08/10/21

For the love of God and my brethren, and in service to them both.
In memory of the lost, forgotten, abandoned, discarded and silenced.
This is also for anyone that I have hurt or discouraged with my words, actions or inaction.
My unworthy testament to Truth & Love.
God loves you, this I know to be true.

Contents

Preface | xiii
Acknowledgments | xvii
Introduction | xix

Truth | 1

A Fresh New Start | 3
A Lie is a Lie | 5
A New Life | 7
A New Star of Light | 8
Be True to You | 10
Because of Him | 12
Change the World | 14
Choices | 15
Circle of Violence | 16
Come Live with Me | 18
Damned | 19
Do I Say What I feel? | 20
Eyes Open | 21
Free Will | 22
God's Love | 23
Good vs. Evil | 25
Immigration | 27
January 6, 2021 | 28

Lamb of God | 29
Losing Your Virtue | 31
Mankind's Demise | 32
More of the Same Insane | 34
My Country | 35
My Holy Stirrup | 36
Puppet on a String | 37
Racism | 40
Racist | 41
Sad & Mad | 42
Satan's Heist | 43
Shed Self & Flourish | 44
Statue | 45
That Crime Way Back in Time | 46
The All-Important Me | 48
The B-Bop Beat of Beelzebub | 51
The Heartbeat Goes On | 52
Time to Live in a Holy Way | 54
Transcendence | 55
Trip to Hell | 57
Truth Speaks | 58
What is a Lie | 60
Without Strife | 62
Woe is Me is its Own Defeat | 64
Yea, But | 65
Your Kingdom Awaits | 66

Love | 69

! | 71
A Love Conundrum | 72
A Love Life | 74
Alone Together | 76
Amor a la Primera Vista | 77
Awake or Asleep | 79
Be Free | 81
Be Love's Superstar | 82
Begging for Love | 84
Breaking Free in Quarantine | 85
By Way of Forgiveness | 88
Dear Departed | 89
Desiring a New Start | 90

¿Despierto o Dormido? | 91
Do It for Love | 92
Do You Really Love Me? | 94
El Silencio Despierta Tu Amor | 96
Grief Stricken | 97
Hide and Seek | 98
Hope | 100
Hypocrisy Destroyed Love | 102
I Love You! | 104
In Love for Love with Love | 107
La Voz de Amor | 109
Live in Love | 111
Llegó el Amor | 112
Love Forevermore | 113
Love is Brand New | 114
Love is My Voice | 116
Love is Waiting in My Heart | 118
Love, m'kay! | 120
Love Whispers | 121
Love's Caviar | 123
Love's Great Escape | 124
Love's Great Roar | 126
Love's Warm Embrace | 127
Maybe We Can Do Better | 129
Ministry of Love | 130
My Heart Beats Again | 131
My Mother | 132
My One-Time, One-of-a-Kind | 135
Ode to the Bygone Days | 138
Peek a Boo | 139
The Mastermind of Love | 140
The Uncle You Can Forget | 141
The Steady Hand of Love | 142
Toxic Love | 144
Welcome to Love | 146
Win My Heart | 148

Light | *149*

A Christian | 151
A Conversation with God | 152
A Conversation with My Soul | 153

All Clear | 155
America Are You Free? | 157
An Evil Pep Rally | 158
Another Day | 160
Be the Light | 162
Be What I Am Meant to Be | 163
Celebrate Life | 165
Confusion | 166
Corona la Llorona | 167
¿Cuál Será Tú Gritó? | 168
Daffodil | 169
Depression Has Lied to You | 170
Down the Rabbit Hole | 172
God, What Would You Have Me Do? | 173
Good Luck Today | 174
Happy Fourth of July | 175
I Pray to be Refined | 176
i want to escape | 177
Jesus Got You | 178
My Kryptonite | 179
Panic in a Pandemic | 181
Perplexed | 183
Self-Absorbed | 184
Senseless Squabbling | 185
Sin | 186
Snooze You Lose | 187
Survivor | 188
The Great Fall | 189
The Light | 191
Transcendence | 192
Tomorrow Today Yesterday | 194
We wait | 196
What a Choice! | 197
Your Right to Fight a Spiritual Rape | 198

Salt | *201*

20/20 Fake and Phony | 203
A House Divided | 205
A Joker | 207
Am I My Brother's Keeper? | 208
America is in Trouble | 211

America's Tit for Tat | 214
Ammo for My Blunderbuss | 216
Anticipating Love | 217
Beyond Hopeless | 218
Blind Sheep | 219
Checkmate | 221
Cold Shoulder | 222
Fake, Fake, Fake | 223
Fake News | 224
Fall Up | 225
Forty-Five | 226
God's Xanadu | 230
Hail to the Mischievous | 231
Historic Virus and a Political Mess | 233
I Will Be Just Fine | 235
I Vote My Faith | 237
In a Pinch? Stop Dancing with That Winch | 238
Life | 239
People Go Crazy | 241
Ramblings of one Sinner to Another | 242
Sin and Guns | 244
Slam on the Brakes | 245
Solitude with Attitude | 246
Start Your Life Anew | 247
The Evil Game | 248
Tragic and Lost | 250
Truth Trumpet | 251
Weak | 253
Well, Well | 255
What Choice in Fallen World | 256
Will We Burn? | 258
Wrong Choices | 259
Yesterday, Today, and Tomorrow I lie | 260

Epilogue | 261

Preface

I believe that most people are not evil, we just make bad choices. At times, awfully bad choices. I have made my share of bad and awfully bad choices! My name, Santos, translates in English to Saints or as the owner of Sasha hair salon in Syracuse, NY once quipped, "Yea, Saint Lucifer." It was a prophetic outburst done in jest that planted a seed in my heart that I was on a treacherous path.

For most of my life I was depressed, lonely and lost. I invited evil into my life at the age of ten, unbeknownst to me. Evil manifested in me both psychologically and physically but it only appeared that I was a sickly and shy child. My spirituality was not attacked, and I was very involved in my church. I grew up across the street from Cristo Rey Parish in Beaumont, TX. From 1980 to 1984 I was the elected president of the Christian Youth Organization; I was an alter boy until I turned eighteen and then organized a young adult group and taught Sunday school for a couple of years.

Although I found love and comfort in church, it only lasted a couple of hours outside of church. I would sink back into my depression and loneliness only to contemplate why I should continue living. Sure, I have some fond and happy memories from this time in my life, but they are few. Mostly I was consumed by worry, loneliness and this overwhelming feeling that I was wandering aimlessly in the dark. Outwardly, I was shy, pleasant and polite. I made good grades and I was not a troublemaker (except for that time in middle school when I secretly removed several paddles from the teachers' classrooms twice and burned them at home with our trash as a silent protest, but I will leave the details of this story for my next book). This kept anyone from really recognizing that I was failing miserably at this thing called life; remember, I was only ten when all this started. For the next seven years I cried out to God every day and every night, begging Him for answers and a cure to what I was experiencing. God, I thought, never answered.

I would not know the truth and depth of my spiritual battle until my forties. One way it controlled my life was through depression and I was a hair trigger away from ending my life several times. At the core of my depression was loneliness even though I had loving and attentive parents, brothers, sisters, friends and other relatives who I knew loved me and cared about me. I was bullied by one person for about a year, but I overcame my fear and stood up for myself at the end, and the bully showed his cowardly true colors like any bully will do without an audience. It was not the physical world that was an obstacle, I was handling this part well, but it was the spiritual. My soul was in agony and my spirit waning.

After several decades of being lonely and miserable, I tired of living in the darkness. One day, as I was contemplating the choices I made up to that point, around 2002, I heard Him clearly speak into my heart saying, "My son, this is not the life I had planned for you." It was so full of Truth and Love that it produced this Light in my heart that slowly brightened with every act of obedience and sacrifice. It put me on a path of righteousness where I walked hand in hand with Christ and allowed Him to guide me to a better place. A place where you experience intimacy with God, and I fell in Love with Him. I had always loved Him, even when I turned away in anger, I never denied His existence nor His majesty, but I fell head over heels in love with Him. Some would love to experience this, but I ask you, what do you do when you can never physically touch or be with your lover? It is a different type of longing than that of a long-distance relationship. It is only through faith, love, and hope that we can be joyful in our relationship with God. Obedience to His will is what I have experienced to be the force behind the grace God showers down on those who seek Him in Truth and Love.

In my debut book, Valiant Cry, I shared a collection of poems inspired by my faith in God. When I collected all the poems inspired over the course of two years, I noticed that they speak of distress and help, God's judgement and His promise of salvation. The title is inspired by Isaiah 33:7. This was also a very fitting description of my spiritual journey where God was molding me like clay on a potter's wheel. I was in a state of re-birth and I was starting to walk upright albeit stumbling and wobbling with a fall here and there but always getting back up no matter the pain and suffering. I continue to grow in love and obedience.

Preface

This book is a continuation of my spiritual journey and a reflection of my experiences of God. Living in Truth and Love in order to live up to what Jesus told us, that we are the Light and Salt of the earth. Right before His ascension into Heaven He was explaining how His disciples would receive the power of the Holy Spirit and that they would be His witnesses to the ends of the earth. This collection of poetry is my effort in faith to discipleship and to witness to this generation, the generation that God chose for me to live in and testify to my experience of God through the beautiful and artful expression of poetry.

Thanks be to God!

Acknowledgments

I would like thank God for leading me to my publisher! Your entire team do wonderful work in the name of Jesus. Thank you so much for believing in me and for your patience with me and my naivety.

I would like to gratefully acknowledge various people who have loved and supported me on my spiritual journey. First and foremost, I would be nothing without the Holy Trinity, thank you for this opportunity to share my experience of You in such an artful way and guiding me through this life. I would also like to express my deep loving gratitude to my parents who always encouraged, supported and never gave up on me. I owe a deep debt of gratitude to my family for your love and support, I love each one of you very much. A special thank you to my brother Gus and my sister-in-law Toni, you opened your home and lovingly cared for me during my recovery from open heart surgery last year and I am forever grateful. I owe a deep gratitude to my cousin Ari, you supported me at the most difficult time in my life when no one else noticed that I needed it, not even myself.

To all my aunts and uncles that have supported and prayed for me, especially Sofia, Lucia, Rosa, Juana, Delma and Pablo.

I owe an enormous debt of gratitude to all of you that encourage me with no self-interest. In pure love you lend your ear and make me laugh and hold my hand when I need it: Austan, Becky, Grace, Juan, Margaret, Meyli and to all my friends at the various stages of my life journey. I am forever grateful to Alma and Carol for your efforts, instruction, support and the opportunity you give me every day to serve my neighbor and by allowing me to flourish in my ministry to serve the community, especially immigrants from twenty-seven different countries.

May God bless all of you that read this book and may His love, grace and mercy fill your heart with joy and peace. May you be inspired in Truth and Love to become Light and Salt of the earth.

Por ti seré, Dios todopoderoso y en memoria del amor y sacrificio de mis padres.

Santos Juan Hernandez, Jr.
Beaumont, TX

Introduction

In my pursuit of an intimate relationship with God, I find myself compelled to share part of my spiritual journey revealing to me gems of wisdom in the form of poetry. These gems are the fruit resulting from my obedience and openness to the inspiration of the Holy Spirit.

Throughout Scripture we are instructed, warned and informed of truth, love, faith, obedience, service, and charity. They are the foundational building blocks of a faith built on rock. The poems I am sharing with you have elements of all these, but I feel in my heart that they are best presented to people of varying levels of faith and non-believers in a way that attempts to, for lack of a better description, reveal the gem's most profound message be it of Truth, Love, Light or Salt.

We are all sinners, and I am no exception. We are all in a different state of Grace or a varying degree of sin, but God's Love and Mercy is immense and infinite. We are all called to Him, we are all invited into eternal Paradise. The only difference is what we do with that invitation. Do we excitedly prepare and await the feast? Do we put away the invitation and forget about it? Do we tear it up as soon as we receive it? The choice is individual, unique to each of us.

Let the gems in this book speak to your heart, let them guide you, let them entice you to a better place and to a place where Truth, Love, Light and Salt take you on your own adventure.

Truth

What is Truth? The age-old question where the elusive but exclusive Truth is exemplified in that very question posed to Jesus by Pilate. As Jesus is revealing to Pilate that He, Jesus, is Truth it only confounds Pilate as he is living only by worldly truths. Pilate, faced with a rebellion and his own political demise, fails to uphold the virtue of Truth. He reveals this in his refusal to initially condemn Jesus as a criminal because he finds Jesus to be an innocent man. He is dissuaded from Truth by fear. Fear that he will lose control of the province; fear that he will lose his political power; fear that he will lose wealth and prestige. There is also an instance where pride rears its ugly head from within Pilate, when he tells Jesus that he alone has the power to put him to death or set him free. As he recognizes the lies of the religious leaders, he fails to recognize the lie that dwells within his own heart which pride obscures.

    We live in similar times because while Jesus conquered death, He conquered it not by revealing Truth to every heart but by inviting us to seek Truth in the Spirit. To be born in the Spirit, to use our faculties to search for truth like Abraham. Our gift of the free will to choose. When Adam and Eve were told not to eat the fruit of the tree of knowledge, they had the free will to decide whether to obey or disobey. We all know what happened. Mankind has evolved, so did technology, while the availability and access of Truth is at our disposal. There was a time that this was not so, where people with power, education, and wealth suppressed truth to lord over the ignorant (or the people without access to the truth by way of worldly means).

There were still those individuals that sought the truth that Jesus spoke of and it was revealed to them, but they were often silenced, murdered, or they were made to disappear.

The Truth is all around us and within us. Truth cannot lie but it must be found in Love, and without Love you cannot possibly recognize the truth. Just as Jesus said, those who seek Truth listen to Him. He also revealed to us who is the father of lies. Today we have the same actor that lied to Eve in the garden serving up lies today challenging the very nature of the truth. No deception of the truth, like he did in the Garden of Eden, but attacking truth itself as a lie because he must reinvent himself in this current age of knowledge. Where knowledge is readily available since Jesus revealed the truth. Today, satan is utilizing the tactic of convincing us that knowledge is what we choose it to be, and this knowledge needs absolutely nothing as a foundation. He further deceives us to accept the premise that truth is subject to this baseless knowledge so it can be distorted and made to satisfy our pride and agenda. His lies tell us that we can make up our own truth and that the truth can change. Listen and accept the devil's lies at your own peril and misery.

The truth is all encompassing, it is basic, and it gives life purpose. Truth is that God loves us, He sent His only Son and the Holy Spirit to reveal the truth of His nature to love.

The Truth Christ delivered will never change, Truth is of God . . . that, you can never exchange!

A Fresh New Start

The amazement and the joy!
I'm no longer the devil's toy
because Jesus has defeated death.
I no longer hide and hold my breath,
I can now shout in the street,
My Lord's resurrection is satan's defeat.
It is by God's love that I am saved,
a golden road is paved,
I just have to turn away from my sin.
Amend my life and be charitable to win!
It is true my Savior lives,
forgives,
and calls us into Love!
Be shrewd but gentle as a dove,
when you go amongst the wolves.
Beware of the devil's evil hooves,
and be open to the Spirit's holy clues
as you spread this Holy news.
God has fixed the problem
of our disobedient conundrum!
He sent His dearly beloved Son,
to pay that egregious ransom.
Now He sits at the Father's right hand,
but does not allow any evil contraband.
Forsake your pride and chide,
for you cannot hide behind that evil snide.
Repent your life of smoke and mirror,
and resist satan's coaxing to come hither.
Persist in this battle for your soul,

all truth be told, Jesus has paid your toll!
Cling to God's Holy Spirit,
draw yourself near it,
He is your only chance to live in truth
and prevents you from being so uncouth.
Lose your worldly heart,
because Jesus has given you a fresh start!

A Lie is a Lie

Liar, liar pants on fire.
Truth be told, lies are for hire,
you hire the lie without any question
you chose it with prideful affection.
All you who shout Jesus help me,
I know you; will you help me?
But Jesus don't know you
You've hired all those lies that define you.
Jesus sees you prefer the lies
hiring one after another with unholy ties.
You compromise Truth for deception,
and lift it up with all your evil affection.
Pride is your game of choice.
Why, you have even lost your voice.
Unrecognizable; lies have changed you,
but the Truth you will never undo.
You misconstrue your virtue
exposing your hypocritical caricature.
So sad that you recognize the lie,
but cover the crime with another lie.
Liar, liar pants on fire
what idle chatter of evil desire.
You fool only yourself,
and the others also in love with himself.
One lie leads to a variety of others
Colorful and dubious druthers.
Jesus and Truth are one
you can't lie about this one hun.

Truth

As much as you can try
A lie, is a lie, is a lie and another lie.
Truth does not change
and does not have an evil range.

A New Life

Hee haw, the mighty fall,
the humble are lifted tall!
The rich go away empty,
and the poor are given plenty!
The proud and loud are silenced.
The meek and peaceful triumphed!
My God, my God is faithful,
and my Lord is truthful!
Redemption and salvation thereof,
but only through true Love!
Turn away from all sin,
and God will insure you win!
Continue to live in sin's ugliness,
and you choose a lonely nothingness!
Love covers a multitude of sin,
today is for your new life to begin!

A New Star of Light

I am aware.
I still cannot hear nor see,
but my soul and spirit are aware of me.
I am connected to love
because I come from love,
not the natural kind you think of
but that of the spiritual kind.
I'm growing each second
meanwhile neurons are firing,
connecting with one another.
I can't wait to hear and see,
but I can feel that you are near me.
I can feel that I am here.
Feeding on love,
and whatever you crave
because there is no running away.
I live because you live.
Floating in an ocean of necessity,
and plugged into the source of vitality.
Only a violent separation
can tear us apart.
Please do not tear me apart,
but maybe my soul was meant to stay home.
Maybe the hate in this world is too much for me.
I hate to think that you just don't love me.

Truth

Maybe, just maybe,
more restraint was in order.
Before he was invited into your sanctity.
Maybe, you should have thought about me, a new life.
A star of the light.
A gift to humanity.

Be True to You

It is in love that you are free,
free from all misery.
While this world careens into chaos,
Jesus accompanies us like He did on the road to Emmaus.
Revealing Himself as we extend an invite,
and teaching us of spiritual delights.
Do not fret or falter,
confess your sins and your life, do alter.
True love you will receive,
while others practice to deceive.
Your life starts anew,
and to sin you bid adieu.
Love will fill your heart,
and a new journey you will start.
Filled with hope and joy,
a new attitude you will deploy.
Praise and proclaim the love of God,
shedding traits like those of Herod.
Become the you God intended,
and find your love and joy extended.
You have placed false hope in this world,
no wonder you feel so cold.
Let love warm your soul,
let God take the center role.
Rejoice and be free,
God makes this promise to thee.
In love you will find your way,
Because Jesus, the Christ, He did pay.
And what did He say?

Love God and neighbor,
in this you will find favor.
Be bold in love,
and as gentle as a dove.
Just like the repenting thief,
you will be freed of this grief.
Your admission secured to Paradise,
because Jesus, well, He paid the price.
All we must become is love,
and do this as gentle as a dove.
Don't get me wrong, this will take practice,
but stop being a thorny cactus.
God is likely to cut you down,
and burn the thorns off your cruel crown.
I often wonder why one wants the thorns,
when God so readily loves and adorns.
Be that loving delight,
and experience True might.

Because of Him

Have you ever tried to count the stars,
or the grains of sand on the beach?
By no means a simple task,
something God simply ignores
when asking us to make that reach,
but not before we relinquish our mask.
The mask of a different you,
the one you put on to confuse and baffle
the very you worth escaping.
An endless feat to renew
our own timeless kerfuffle
of a meaningless spiritual draping.
It surmises to say
that if you are loveless,
you wander through life lost and found.
You admire hearsay,
become enthralled with nonetheless,
and to doubt you are bound.
Why try to count the sand and stars?
Because of promises and covenants
made by Truth and Love.
Those made by God who heals all scars,
and removes all of evil's remnants,
showering you with Love's treasure trove.

Truth

A mighty task
which requires a fast,
an obedience,
and another chance.
I beg you to turn to prayer.
Ignore the evil naysayer,
dispel that worthless despair,
and reclaim your status as a holy heir.

Change the World

Be eager to be free
  And you will see
    A better world this could be
      Love and smile with me
        For this brings a guarantee
          A brighter future for our society!

Choices

There once was a mother known as Eve
   yet she would soon fall to the deceive.
Her spouse was happy to oblige and rise
     to bite and to swallow
        an evil hypnotize.
A new Mother selected in full favor
   chosen to bring forth our Creator.
Her spouse this time hesitant
  a dream
     an Angel
       a full-on participant.
Worlds apart these two sets of parents
   one disobedient, and prideful declarants
     the other humble, unselfish and kind.

The latter would help save mankind
   the differences are quite clear
      the temptation whispered in your ear
        to which will you draw near?
                A choice to disobey.
                A choice to obey.

          This choice runs endlessly every day.

Circle of Violence

Saying I love all of you today
only fades away
when the moon goes down
and the sun comes up.
Another day.
In this world temporary rules
wait until tomorrow and I will call you all fools!
Today, love can rule but tomorrow?
Another day.
This love thing is fleeting,
and you buy into the misleading.
You think you know it all
But you don't care at all,
much less about your fall.
Another day.
I'm fed up with these pretenses
are you people out of your senses?
To hell, you say, to your offenses.
Another day.
Why are you so angry?
Why it was just yesterday
that you loved without delay.
But only because it brought attention your way
but today you say
shut up!
Another day.

So, on day one you must choose love,
and day two you move
to a groove seemingly smooth.
But then you run and dash to your balderdash!
Another day.
And so on and so on
the circle of violence be done to everyone.
Unless, of course, you break that circle of violence today.
Then you will see a brighter day!

Come Live with Me

I thought I should tell you,
when I say I love you
this does not excuse the evil you do.
Believe Me, I would hate to say adieu.
I would prefer and love to save you!
You shouldn't take my mercy for granted,
one day I will allow you to be taunted,
haunted and feeling defaulted.
It is your love I seek in return,
not some burn,
or some evil turn.
Without a heavenly yearn.
I want you to be reborn!
Not living of this worldly porn.
I want to adorn, not scorn.
Ultimately it comes to free will.
Are you seeking the worldly cheap thrill,
or are you searching for something real?
Let me offer you this deal
You love me completely,
and your neighbor equally,
and I will treat you respectfully.
Choose Me,
and this Holy Trinity
will lead you to eternity,
to live with Me.

Damned

When light came to be,
the dust and clay were made life.
Perfection in a body,
which today felt no strife.

Darkness betrayed the Almighty,
snuffing out the model's life.
Time stood still while moving slowly,
people suffered and died but still no chosen wife.

Evil continued to enjoy the party,
but true to Truth a Mother, a lowly midwife.

A holy continuity.

The veil torn midlife.

Salvation for humanity.

Most believing the lies of the magic fife,
damned becomes their eternity.

Do I Say What I feel?

Do I Feel What I say?

One thing is said
Another thing is felt
One thing is felt
Another thing is said

Do they ever come together?

We are free to choose
How will I feel?
What will I say?

Can it be that I don't care either way?

Only thing that matters is
How will I feel?
What will I say?
What can I live with?

Especially if they are not the same.

Eyes Open

Beware the snare
of the devil's evil glare
Once deceived
You cannot conceive
the difficulty
of being aware
of your faculty
Much less
aware
of your spirituality.

Free Will

You do not have to listen to me that God created humanity
Yes, you can say it is one big mystery
faith is our history and Love is the believer's ministry
It is easy for us to believe in eternity
being the masterpiece of God's creativity
because Truth is planted in our spirituality
You must place your trust in the Holy Trinity
It is your right to fight this reality
as the devil tempts your will to be but only leads you to a travesty
To be or not to be is the question demons ask of thee
and only you can foresee your own desire to be a queen bee
whether it is too late to hear the banshee
Better you decree that you believe in the Holy Trinity
and forsake your pride because you see it is only by spirituality
that you can fully be what God intended you to be

Profess your love in the Holy Trinity
and the Holy Spirit will lead you to eternity!
Deny this Truth for proclivity in human negativity
and you will surely suffer the same fate as the wickedly
by joining in their twisted ministry of vanity.

God's Love

Looking down at the angry face of fear with arms stretched out,
    nailed and in pain He never yelled out
                                      You Fools!
It was love which reigned through all that blood
    being spilled in order to renew.
The glorified priests jeered that they needed proof
    because they cannot believe their hearts,
        and it doesn't make any sense with all their smarts.
As the blood flowed from his open flesh,
    He suffered to take in every breath,
        but He endured the pain to let us know He was true.
Every ugly, violent and cruel thing we could do,
    He loved us still through all the fear, pain and hate.
Could you do the same?
Or would you be a bit irate?
Would you take satan's bait?
Would you be filled with hate,
    for those that nailed you to the cross?
What about your Mother as she looked on?
Dead and buried, in His Mother's arms, she did not scorn
    those that killed Her Son like He was nothing to no one.
Even when He reached His throne,
    He did not wreak havoc on all those that did Him harm,
        and scorned the love of His Father with our disobedience and arrogance.
Together they instead released their Spirit of Love
    onto a creation enslaved by lies and deceit.
And you are still having trouble believing.
Are you still in satan's court sneering?

Even now He loves and forgives,
> He only asks that we love and forgive.

A much better price than selling our soul
> to a devil that only desires to control.

Good vs. Evil

The Spirit tells you to pray
but you choose to go astray.
satan whispers sweet nothings,
and you run to act like human offerings.
Are we human, yes!
But this is one great game of chess.
Pride goes before the fall,
so don't be so fast to stand so tall.
Obedience leads you to serve others,
it is not in your interest to harm your brothers.
When the devil comes a knocking,
remember it is he who is also mocking.
Become the child God created in you,
be born in the Spirit and live your life anew.
Lose your life and gain it forever,
love this life only means the devil was more clever.
Hold on tight,
because this is a spiritual fight.
The battle draws near your heart,
this was the case from the very start.
Eve with her no, while Adam followed,
let death enter the world disavowed.
Mary and Joseph with their yes,
allowed a Heavenly redress.

So, what I say to you today,
is to not be led astray.
Turn from that evil way,
and feed that devil dismay!
God will smile,
and will receive you in Heavenly style!

Immigration

Immigration, the new but old hate libation
      Indulging in the liberation of a sinister side
Don't try to hide the tide of this tsunami of lies
      Incredibly intolerant to their or their babies' cries.
Their cries will capture His ears and so will your fears
      All because we believe the devil's jeers and sneers
We focus too much on judgmental arrears
      using this wealth of pirated lies to divide
           and confuse in all its regal pride
We are empowered to rebuke this ruse
      by choosing to love
           hope and serve
                  those we choose to abuse

January 6, 2021

This is what lies can do,
what one man's pride can do.
Disrupting our democratic Xanadu.
While people die
because of the herd lie,
forty-five continues to pile on the lie.
What a shameful act,
inciting this treasonous act
and that, is an evidenced fact.
You who approve
are dancing to the puppeteer's move
hemming and hawing lies, and his term did conclude
while his lie is fodder to his sheep,
completely asleep,
while forcing that lie on others in a heap.
Not since our past enemy burned down the Capitol
have we had an enemy done something so tyrannical
and their leader, forty-five occupies the oval all hysterical.
This circus master sits in the People's castle
refusing to go home, and popping some evil capsule,
still trying to frazzle.
Fear is the game,
Fear is the shame,
Fear makes all of you just so very lame.
The only thing that will save you is Love.

Lamb of God

His will relinquished
as He prays and sweats blood, intended.
A terrible fear of the desert dreaded,
craving the true love upended.
Arrested and abandoned,
beaten, spat upon, and humiliated.
His body vanquished,
His spirit tested.
Paraded in His misery for all to see,
we mock, ridicule, and yell obscenity.
We are the fools evil laughs with, in glee.
Yet, He maintains calmly and quietly.
Pride, fear, and greed rule the day,
as He, peaceful as a dove is led away.
To the death! We all say.
While He thinks, what a glorious day.
His body nailed on a stake of wood,
while God's priests in pride they stood.
Jesus gasps for air, no one understood
only He, the Son, could.
Evil laughs as His last drop of blood spills
and those in power, bloated pride chills.
God has other plans, as His Son wills.
Love wins and you hear all the devil's shrills.
Recall Love's power
when all you can do is cower,
and call upon God's truth tower,

Jesus Christ, the ultimate love sower!
He is raised to life,
ending forever evil's strife.
He grants a divorce from pride's wife,
and opens a path to Heaven's Paradise.

Losing Your Virtue

Once you surrender your soul
you lose control.
Question is, who pays the toll?
Give it to the liar
you will hurt and become the crier.
Give it to the Truth
and you will grow in strength.
People will fight for control of you,
they will misconstrue and obscure
the real you.
Only true love can save you,
to keep you from getting screwed
and losing your virtue.

Mankind's Demise

A Christian in name only,
what an evil phony.
A cacophony of lies and deceit,
just hate filled baloney,
provoking the illicit paradigm of spiritual sanctimony.
You are what Christ warned would feed on the rind,
of the unconscious mind.
We were warned that in a future time,
a sublime character would rise and blind mankind.
Many will bind their mind to a lying mastermind.
It is happening in your own mind,
not outside to all the rest of humankind.
In your own heart Christ is inclined,
to lead you to the true sublime,
of the Heavenly kind!
You must unravel that evil in your mind,
and pray a little.
A lot more if you ignore,
or abhor it as a chore.
Harden not your heart or the mind,
rebuke those pursuits of evil intertwined,
or suffer your own demise
for the failure to recognize,
the evil and the lies of the liar's mastermind.
Your only saving grace from eternal disgrace
is that race to serve in love, for love's sake.

Unfortunately, like we were told,
most will continue to be fooled
and live a lie,
choosing willfully to be fake
even while knowing what is at stake.

More of the Same Insane

What's on my mind?
All of the unkind!
I'm unkind,
others are unkind
it all blows my mind!
Over and over and rewind,
turn around and more of the unkind.
Everywhere there's more of the same,
all this angry stew of the insane
like it is one big mocking game.
No matter if we cause another pain,
we just blame, blame and shame.
Stirring up toil and trouble,
always preparing to scuffle
so the truth can take a tumble.
We engage in the rudest hustle
just so we can hear the other cry uncle.

My Country

When I was told as a boy
  as a man, life is no toy
    you can do as you say
      because people have paved the way.
You can say what you say with no one taking that away.
You can live free to pursue your dream
  due to the life of an airman, a soldier, a sailor and marine.
With a true spirit of brotherhood,
  they stood,
    not to brood but because they could!
It takes a certain type of person to join
  not no flip of a coin!
It is understood amongst this kind,
  amidst all our struggles, they find
    what is in their mind,
      is blind to the grind,
        they fight for humankind.

        Should a people be so inclined?
        To live as free as these heroes have enshrined?

My Holy Stirrup

Eeeny
       meeny
             miny
                  mo
                    My spirit is oh so po,

                 Help me Jesus get back up,

                 and be my holy stirrup!

Puppet on a String

I open my eyes and listen for my marching orders,
  Can I dress now?
    Can I eat?
      Can I breathe?
        Can I think of my disorder?
I can't be me, whomever that may be.
  I don't control what I can think.
    Who did this to me?!
      Don't you see?
        You are the problem with me!
Me, myself, and I,
  Oh, what a high!

Can't get me out of my head
  Not even in bed, when I fall to sleep.
    I hope to dream about me and mine.

Even in love it is about what I love,
  never is it about true love loving.

For love's sake, yes, even the unkind.
  I would rather seek out the fake
    in everything I take into my mind,
      tuck it into my heart and unwind
        those strings that tell me what to think, say and do.
          I then dare to wish for a new start?!

I see and hear people
  but I do not hear what they are talking about,
    much less pay attention to what they do.

Maybe, just maybe, this is how I got into this mess with me and you.
  Ignoring the sanity in my heart that transfers to my head,
    instead, I run to the next bullhorn of nothings being said.

An empty voice full of hopeful lies,
  while my spirit slowly dies.
    I can't say I was not warned
      But I only wanted the truth I wanted to be true for me and you.
        Because I want to think for you,
          just as I gave up my mind and soul
        I want you to be just as bold!
          In giving up your soul.

Listen to the make-believe
  that manipulates and deceives
    the likes of which you cannot see
      before it's too late, do you see?
        Maybe I never will, but it's never too late
          to take back what was stolen
            or that I gave up for free.

Maybe, just maybe,
  there is still hope for me
    but only if I choose love
      and not hate, judgement, or lies.

This implies that I was wrong,
   and maybe I don't dare admit
      that I was wrong
         and not strong enough to control
            my own habitual habit
               of tying myself up
                  like a puppet on a string.

Racism

R ecycle
A ngry
C owardly
I gnorant
S inful
T houghts

Racist

R eprehensible
A pathy
C owardly
I nstigates
S ocietal
M alfeasance

Sad & Mad

When hopes and dreams are shattered,
When young and old don't seem to matter,
What does this say about our chatter?
Hate, lies, rudeness and more of the latter!
Nothing will change until we change.
Maybe you say I'm not to blame,
What a shame!
We can all do better.
We can start by not using the young and old as victim fodder
To score points on one another!
The real solution?
Eliminate the hate pollution
Collaboration and collusion.
Believing you are better than any other!
Or that you deserve more than your brother!

Satan's Heist

What lies have you accepted for truth?
That everyone else is wholly uncouth?
While you offer yourself an excuse.
Not only you, but also others that accuse.
In the name of God, you claim your pride,
At least Adam & Eve were right to hide.
But yours is a more evil state,
Going from hate to hate.
Never satisfied by any evil endeavor,
You just march on into death forever.
Staring at your brother & wishing him ill,
While, in the name of peace you yell kill!
Look into the looking glass of honesty,
What you see is distorted hypocrisy.
Distorted in its loving stare,
You don't even notice satan's glare.
You only see what you want to see,
A perfectly perfect righteous me.
What deception causes you to believe,
Is that truth is what you perceive.
This is why you don't try to listen,
All you tout is that I am a good Christian.
Far from the truth you have strayed,
I wonder what happens to all those prayers you have prayed.
Back to the core teachings of Christ,
Is the only way to remedy satan's heist!

Shed Self & Flourish

In order to be free listen to my plea,
refrain from the pain of disdain.
Find hope in the seemingly mundane,
and find your reign
in the hope of the Holy Trinity again!
Don't hold true what you hear from a mere man
without spreading your wingspan,
and relying on God's masterplan!
Otherwise, you are led astray to your dismay.
You need a game plan.
One that doesn't rely on an anchor man,
nor a helmsman,
or some false clergyman, or businessman
much less a politicking man.
What you need is the main fisher of man!
Only on Him rest your eyes,
and look towards the prize; it is no surprise
He gives salvation to the wise,
and to those who heed His call
to chastise self
in the worldly,
and become Holy.
Despise the lies of the unwise.
Surmise, you live baptized!
In the Holy Blood of our beloved.
Now this, this can be coveted.

Statue

What is a statue but concrete or metal, glass, marble or some other type of matter? Does it breathe, does it have any life other than the life we think it honors or a moment in time best forgotten, ill-gotten, or even to make amends? What glory does it have if we have forgotten to love and care for the downtrodden? We tear them down, but we leave up the structures in our minds not knowing that it binds us to it even as it comes down. We protect them with our guns while we kill others for fun or just because we don't like someone. We rape, pillage and plunder our own people, none of us deserve a statue. Mankind is unkind and we thought this country was coming along from the days we treated people worse than dogs, but lo and behold the racists have become bold, and everyone else is becoming cold. We claim to be the best, but when put to the test we are better than the rest at revenge, and the statues we create, as that appendage to a cause ill-gotten or forgotten because we obscure the topic, stand tall and proud in a lost crowd. Play your evil games, and dance with the devil, but don't cry and wail when the ship sets sail without your kind becoming like that statue, just a speck in time. Turn to love and let it drive your mind, it will turn you away from being unkind, and you break free and live for all time; greater than the statue which only lived in someone's mind, before it was carved and shaped from matter that has no spirit in it.

That Crime Way Back in Time

What is the crime of all time?
Do you really have to ask?
Let me provide a hint in rhyme,
Don't get lost, you have only one task
To read past these first few lines!
There were really two crimes in total
One almost caused a failed betrothal
The other, in the beginning
Succeeded in the bleeding.
The crime in that time, there were two.
The first enticing the following coup.
A whisper in the ear of my sister.
A beautiful liar but far more sinister.
He caressed her ear
with an intoxicating, "come here."
She knew better.
She was told to the letter,
Do not touch or taste of just this one.
This was too easy; she wanted a throne.
When my brother came searching,
she became the temptress besmirching.
He, curious about holding a golden rod,
decided to go along, disobeying God.
Now you've gone and done it!
Between the three, a crime of deceit.
No, you cannot take it back.
You must pay, and sadly, death is like crack!
More and more, forevermore,
but God had to settle that devil's score.

Truth

What no one can see
is God's plan for you and me.
Only God knows what would repair
man's self-inflicted disrepair.
His Son agreed to leave His throne,
To humble Himself, bemoan
in a worldly agony
with a message found in Deuteronomy
Chapter twenty-eight to be exact.
You can still find it intact,
the very fine act of Heavenly allegiance.
We must all desire complete obedience
to love God above all, and with our all.
To love each other, as the first install.
Love and obedience will take over,
and death will never hover,
because Jesus has conquered death
when sin took His last breath,
but that same death had no power
over God's grace and mercy shower!
God's plan revealed
as satan squealed.
There was never a question of if God
would come to the rescue of the synod,
but when He would find that one to say yes.
That Virgin who would not stray.
That one, that man who trusted,
and could not be busted.
He finally found those two.
The two that helped in saving me and you.
The ones who were true and true.
Obedient in faith and love so sure.
That they helped God repair that crime
way back in time.

The All-Important Me

If I see the all-important me,
I wonder why everyone else cannot see
how important it is to be me.
I wake up and manage my struggles
while everyone else is losing their scruples.
I have an answer to everything
but I wonder why no one ever asks me anything.
It must be some conspiracy!
I am sure everyone has heard of me.
It's not as if I am resisting transparency.
If you ask me, the all-important me,
I could improve this world we live in
because even my opinions have profound meaning.
Just imagine tapping into my mind!
It would get us out of every bind.
I don't even want to start on my heart
but I can tell you this, it is very smart!
I cannot fathom why we need
any other idea or all this greed
to be more like me.
This world only needs the all-important me.
Why, you could not handle the struggle
and would just bungle it all up.
You were not fortunate to be like me.
Now, let us take a dose of reality.
In a fallen world this all important me
is the source of all hypocrisy,
envy, lust, pride and gluttony.
We, that is you and me,
all start to think like the all-important me,

and where does this lead us on our shared journey?
A corrupt and greedy feeding frenzy!
Feeding on the hearts and minds of people blinded,
by the glamour of the all-important me
where it gets all dressed up in idolatry
enticing and inviting you to that all important me.
That this will somehow bring you dignity.
I'm sorry to say you have been led astray,
but it is not too late to mend your way.
This all important me is but a ruse
for satan to amuse
by our lack of thinking of anything besides ourselves.
He is the original all important me
conceiving the notion,
and then perfecting his evil commotion
enticing us to drink his toxic "me" potion.
Your only cure and disruption
of his diabolical plan
is to give yourself the upper hand,
a devotion to a righteous plan.
The one God said would save our soul,
a Shepherd's goal to win your soul.
A commitment and life lived in Love,
the love of our Father from above
who sent His only Son
to pry us from this all important me,
and to draw us to a confraternity
of a Heavenly and Divine family!
The Father and Son sent their Spirit
to teach, enlighten and guide.
All I must do is open my heart,
and invite Him to live in it.
This will destroy this prideful arrogance
paraded by that all important me,
and lead us to a joyful and peaceful free.

A state of being like no other,
the freedom and desire to love my brother!
The world would be a better place,
and we would race,
to love each other.

The B-Bop Beat of Beelzebub

be blind,
be bound,
be boastful,
be belligerent,
berate,
belittle,
beguile,
be biased,
be brazen,
bicker,
be bitter,
be broken,
blaspheme,
banish,
be baneful,
bewitch,
be bitchy,
be blistering,
be brooding,
be bleak,
bully,
bemuse,
be bad,
be brilliantly bad!

The Heartbeat Goes On

So, the beat goes on.
What I heard in that room,
I thought I was gone.
Professionals synchronized,
and aggressively had to pass the baton.
Dr. Oz and his team delivered beautifully.
A Christmas card and a prayer until this life is done.
It is the least I could do for that life he won.
I take this life too much for granted,
although I was ready to see Mom, Dad,
God, Jesus, Mary, and all the rest
God has a different plan.
One where I must take a stand to be my best.
Picture is not clear, especially right now,
while I'm swollen, cut, stapled together,
full of drugs, and other people's blood.
I have a long road ahead,
and it will not be easy.
Some people God has shown me
to be alright,
while others, for the best,
have taken flight.
It's alright this sort of sorts.
Better than holding out hope,
for that one who thinks life is a joke,
when this haze lifts and I learn to walk.
In the meantime, I must let others speak
about what they want to do to help me.

Especially when I want to do the helping,
but when your chest is cut wide open,
there's not much but broken.
I know it is no small token,
God's love for me,
because you see, I was walking around
working & talking, but with the sinister lurking.
Since there were four veins blocked ninety-nine percent,
I'm a miracle to be here, now a bit reticent,
and we miss these too often.
Calling them luck or just being fortunate.
When I think of the minute details
leading up to this day
it blows my mind away.
God is with us every minute of every day.
He is the only reason things turned out OK.

Time to Live in a Holy Way

Time to pray and live in a holy way.
Time also to call all those who lost their way.
This is a test of faith and love of neighbor.
This is not the time to protest and waver.
Love covers a multitude of sin.
God knows you from within.
As a people, we must feel the pain of others,
and comfort our brothers.
This is a test of the spiritual network.
Time to pray, fast,
and be torqued from our sinful past.
Good thing Jesus said
I am with you to the end, and so is my Dad.
Do not fear, it is only here
that is temporary my dear.
We all must go one day
but for most it will not be today.
Beware when this too shall pass
because you, loving others, will have to last!

Transcendence

I search for relevance
While I experience
A society's heart addicted to decadence
I ponder the elegance
Of love and forgiveness
In a world that demands evidence
Beyond a preponderance
That life is no happenstance
While we all live by chance
In the fog of a prideful arrogance
Brought upon us by the naive brilliance
Of a people eager to serve reluctance
With such eloquence
And with an ill-conceived persistence
Eager to the dominance
Of forces that demand crassness
Because it enslaves righteousness
And lays waste all truthfulness
To the acceptance
Of hopelessness
But then there is a Light of excellence
That shines in brightness
Which beckons one with openness
And invites us to fruitfulness
With a peaceful awareness
That captivates our playfulness
And eradicates any boastfulness
But rather excites the humbleness
Of our soul and a mindfulness

That we do not exist in aloneness
But we coexist in oneness
And are invited to an eternal blissfulness
And the devil's lie is not life's existence
We should love to reach a fullness
And completeness
A transcendence
Otherwise, life is just a fretful trance

Trip to Hell

All be told, it's pretty bold!
Going into your enemy's domain.
Jesus was not going down to scold,
nor was He to remain.
Jesus is Savior to all of mankind,
not just the living at that time.
He stepped into hell, in order to rewind
death's spell because of satan's crime.
Imagine the joy upon His arrival!
All those souls that the devil kept bound,
Jesus let all there know, there has been a reprisal!
God has not forgotten you, for you have been found.
Although He went, there is a requirement.
Because your will is still free,
do you accept this invite to God's holy firmament?
Or would you rather satan's crime spree?
This was the trip He took to unbind the chains of sin.
Can you believe, some would say no?
You had the chance, once again, to begin.
Jesus, I imagine, said to all the faithful I told you so,
God had a plan to save you,
it is time to go!
Bid hell and satan a big adieu,
for I have saved you!

Truth Speaks

Don't you see me?
I am not invisible you see,
you just do not acknowledge Me.
Then you say what's wrong today
where am I to show you the way?
Claiming you are too busy anyway.
Then tragedy strikes,
and you yell YIKES
wondering where you went astray,
listening to this world betray
My Love and devotion.
What did you think would come of all this commotion?
That I can save you from your choices,
when I gave you possession of your voices?
You choose to snooze,
and you drink the booze
of lies and deception
forsaking my intercession
thinking it a molestation
all this truth oration.
Then you dare ask what becomes of your nation?
History ignored because you are bored,
but it has all been foretold
that when you ignore Me
I let you be
leaving you to your vices
until you realize the prices!
But no prizes.

I hope you are not too late,
to ignore hate.
Turn to Me, and conquer the crises.
Turn away, and the liar's device arises
and you finally feel the weight of hate
                              berate.

What is a Lie

I've been told that a lie is white, black, gray, evil and good.
This is food for thought,
but can a lie be good?
So I'm sitting here, deep in thought
A lie can be thought, bought and sold.
This is true.
A lie can expand or complete a plan.
This is true.
A lie can live alone and promote its own.
This is true.
A lie can live in ambiguity for perpetuity.
This is true.
A lie without being shy, can deny any lie.
This is true.
A lie will most often promote fear.
This is true.
A lie rooted in pride, will distort and hide.
This is true.
A lie convinces that one thing is another.
This is true.
A lie is fixated on deception,
and misconception.
This is true.
A lie peddles itself as a truth.
This is true.
A lie exalts and proclaims its own aim.
This is true.
A lie has its own native tongue.
This is true.

A lie is a cheater and a repeater.
This is true.
A lie has no character, it is his own master.
This is true.
A lie usually leads to another lie.
This is true.
A lie can be good if it is shrewd,
that is a lie, this is not true!

Without Strife

You can have what I have too!
This love that runs through and through
God is looking to share it with you!
He waits every day, until you make your way,
making that commitment not to stray!
I'm all in, is what He wants to hear you say.
You get all hyped and then satan strikes,
convincing you that there were no spikes,
but tempts you over to what he likes!
Your demise on the horizon, he goes full blown.
Making you believe you are all grown, or alone!
No need to fret, get rid of that frown.
Raise your eyes to heaven and wail,
oh God, I am so frail
from all this evil ale.
The devil has me believing his tall tale!
God will answer your prayer.
He will send the Holy Spirit, the evil slayer,
and restore you in front of the naysayer!
He loves and cherishes you,
but you must love Him too
so that He can bless you,
and then stick to Him like glue!
Believe me, for I know this to be true.
I was once so blue,
and when I was only twenty,
satan had me believing that pain was plenty.
I put a gun in my mouth,
ready to blow my brains south.

Truth

It was love that made me back down.
The devil laughed, and jeered, your such the clown.
God picked me up, wiped my tears,
and gave me heavenly cheers,
but it took years.
And here I am, praising His name!
This is no game.
Only God and you want the same
eternal life,
without the strife!

Woe is Me is its Own Defeat

Precarious is the spiritual wariness that makes you believe the lure of satan's pestilence. It seems a mess, this idleness of woe is me, why can't he let me be? He lives to disturb my destiny. He whispers these sly innuendos, exhorting worldly pleasure crescendos. I can't help but hear him always ready to feed me deceit, enchanting me with the comfort of defeat. It is in the tiniest of deceptions that he gains in your affections. Be on guard against this seemingly innocuous offensive gesture used only to pester you into a life of make believe! Be relieved that there is a cure and protection against the master of evil posture, giving to you is the gift of evil's detection. You must claim this as with any prize, to thwart your demise call upon the name on high this everlasting King of mine! Yours too, if you so choose, just proclaim it loud and sure, that you will honor this truth God the Father, God the Son, and God the Spirit only if you are with it will this save your soul and spirit!

Yea, But

Yea, the Romans crucified many,
but they built a modern society.

Yea, Pharaohs enslaved the masses,
but cannot deny the pyramid's vastness.

Yea, Aztecs tore out hearts of the living,
but with science and technological winning.

Yea, Nazi's built camps of concentration,
but they modernized fabrication.

Yea, America enslaved and killed nations,
but we modernized civilizations.

Yea, we love espousing the good,
but we remain silent on the rude.

Yea, we pray and go to church,
but we fail in love as the evil lurch.

Yea, we live to die and rise,
but we live and lie, to our soul's demise.

Your Kingdom Awaits

Will you go My Son?

Yes Father, I will go to them,
and share with them what You have said.

They will not believe You,
only the few that I will send to You.
Some will believe but then turn away,
violently but be not afraid.

That's ok Father, I will love them anyway.

Remember, that is the devil's playground,
and he can lie his way around love.
Making them fear, loath, and doubt.

I trust in your plan Father,
I know your love stands,
and though they may fall away
most of them will love You anyway.

My Son, You are the One.
My Advocate that I told to the Prophets.
You will not have much time with them,
to share Our love and reveal their pride.

I can do it Father because I love them
as You love them, and I will come back.

My Beloved Son,
I will miss You so much, but I am here
waiting for You my dear Boy.

I trust you Father,
because I watched when You made them,
and breathed Your Spirit into them.
I was right next to You in love, and We fell in love with them.

This trip will test You My Son,
but We have no choice
satan has ravished them with lies,
and contributes to their demise
with more and more lies.

I agree, Father, it is time.
You have picked a true Mother
that will choose Your love
when Gabriel tells Her of Your move
in this love affair with mankind.
I will obey and bide My time,
until You say "It is time, My Son,
evil has won this round but just wait
You will rise again!"
I love You Father!

I love You My Son!
I will see You soon.
Just look to the moon if you need to remember that I created You too.
Don't let satan convince You that I have nothing to do with You.
That love in Your Heart was put there by Me. Tell them I did the same for them,
they just have to trust in what I've said
not all that confusion the devil put in their head,
because they wanted to be led.

Tell them I'm the One who sets them free,
to choose Me in love,
and then lead others to me in love.
Not by force or coercion, but in love
and hope to be reunited with Me.
You will feel dejected when I must turn away from all their sin.
You must pick up, and carry, in the form of a cross.
Remember My Son, You belong to Me,
and I will raise You up to rule beside Me.
All those that give up their lives on that devil's playground,
and choose the truth in love You told, will also be reunited with me!
Go now in haste,
there is no time to waste.
Your kingdom awaits Your coming!

Love

Ah, Love! Everyone craves, longs, and searches for it. We want to be loved, and desire to love others. We all have our own idea of love, even those who suffer abuse or those who feel all alone even those that say no one loves them. Some are giddy in love, some comfortable, some excited and others exhausted. Some even feel overwhelmed by the challenges love poses. I was a lost soul for a great part of my life. I knew of Love, but I was never aware that the Love I was familiar with, that which existed in my mind, was not really love at all. What I did not realize is that without knowing true love, the love in my heart was this distorted existence of love which fogged and obstructed my ability to comprehend true Love. My love had expectations and requirements attached to it. I found myself looking for love in all the wrong places, mainly through the lens of pride, lust, vanity, and destructive desire.

Love is Love, you cannot expect or require anything for it. It is not a commodity to be bought, sold, bartered and traded like the world would have you believe. Love is at the very core of our being, our soul. We come from Love itself, God. Therefore, we are lost without God because we are in constant search for our home in love, in God. This is the cup that Jesus was trying to pass that night in the Garden of Gethsemane, being separated from Love itself, our God. He prayed three times to have it pass, but He knew that it was only through Love that mankind would be saved and reunited with God. Jesus surrendered His will to God, because of His Love for all of us past, present and future. Look at all He endured for love of God and us.

Love is a complex simplicity. I love you. Three words, and only two other words reflect the depth of God's love for us, Jesus wept. Love is obscured by millennia of sin, evil, our fallen spirit and within our very soul. We throw up our hands and look away, having become indifferent to the likes of love, and thus, to Truth. Without love there can be no truth. Without love, there can only exist a mirage of faith. Without love there can be no joy. Without love, the only hope we desire are the acquisition and attainment of worldly things. Without love, we allow the satan to entice and endear us with lies to lead us away from God. Just as we want the answer to what is Truth, why don't we ask what is love? We take it for granted that we must all be familiar or to know of love intimately through those three simple words, I love you.

Love, in its truest nature is existing in an intimate relationship with God. It is only through this relationship that we are granted access to love and to also receive love. Anything short of this is cheating yourself to a worldly knockoff. Your heart becomes a maze of mirrors, not knowing which expression is real. Love is not an emotion but an existence, a state of joyful and peaceful hope in the Resurrection, absent of all malice. Love means we care, we empathize, we share, we help, we provide, we are compassionate, we nurture, we are gentle, sympathize, we honor, we are just, and we forsake the evil of the satan within us. There is no more powerful a virtue or gift than the Love God bestows upon you when you ask, seek, or knock.

It is only through Love that we can live forever, prepare yourself for this endeavor!

!

Do not lose hope today!
   Love still exists in every way!
    Love has defeated hate in every which way!
     Love has been crowned with glory in all ways!
      Love is still our go to in hard times and struggle anyway!
       Don't let the raging loud noise of hate and destruction
        make you think that we love any less today!

Hate just has a louder noise while love silently and humbly prevails each day!
   While voices of hate and division get all the airway,
    we the people, love in simple, humble, and in a huge way!
    Don't let your love waste away!
     Don't allow despair to win the day!
      Pray anyway, love every day!
       Let love lead your way!
        Be kind and smile to everyone this day!

A Love Conundrum

Heartbroken, but no one knows because what shows outward are only the unknowns of bygone ghost towns trying to show something normal and desirable. Only I know the truth that lies inside, or do I? Filled to the brim with love but who would know? It is all bottled inside the mind of the heart, all settled in, underneath the cork with no way to depart but wanting to shout. Even if I did shout who will hear it if I allow no one near it? If I do shout it is only in whispers. Is it me or what else could it be? Will I ever discover how I entered this bottle of something so subtle, where I see out and others see in, but ever apart from each other? And who was it that pressed the cork in so deep that only that unique and intriguing screw could force it out without tearing me apart? I listen to a melodic tune of want and desire, but do I hide from what I really think is not mine? Undeserving of the crime of stealing someone's heart because I think I am the only one in need of this love? Even if they offer it up for free because it is in the nature and glee of their life, does it really belong to me? Is this why I locked myself away? So as not to reward my lover with the real me, since I only guess as to who this can really be, an empty or complicated persona? Maybe all I can muster is this illusion of a real me, too tainted by the memory of a past life or future strife not even lived...only perceived. Or maybe, just maybe others may see what they want to see. The real me! Could this be that love is so powerful that it sees through that fog of self-doubt, and can only see what lies in my heart? Without a thought, true love, falling in love with me can break through, wanting to find me because it sees me as their saving grace behind the glass. Break in case of an emergency! What they see is different than what I see of me. I only stare at a reflection instead of what is on the other side of that clear glass with no distortion or obstruction. If they be so courageous with their love, can I return the favor? Is my love recognizable since I am unfamiliar with it, or is it unfamiliar? Confusion would be an excuse at my age with experience, but I use it like a crutch. Could it be called fear to draw near? Thus, the glass to see but never touch? This love thing is a weird thing, demanding but submissive only adds to the intrigue of a desire to be wanted by that love that is exactly right and burning bright. Just on the other side of the glass leaving me filled with inexplicable delight in the knowing, it is right. Is Love always winning the fight? So I decide to surrender to love's might at my midnight, but do I waste time looking behind? Wondering what life could have been like if only I did this at my dawning light? Since true love demands your attention, I guess it doesn't matter because you can only go along for the ride or spend your spent energy trying to hide out in the open. It is difficult to understand when baggage makes a formidable stand, but can you control who falls in love with you? And can I extinguish the flame of the love in me returning to thee? Why would I want to?! Is it even worth the Inquisitor's glance to dance with the unknown only meant to distract? All my life, I think I always longed the complete and true love of another, but I convinced my heart that I needed no other. Time to face the fact that love, in real terms, cannot be put asunder! It is like thunder but not with the same fright, this fear is unclear and is more like a new start for the heart. One filled with wonderful delight in really knowing each other like no other. Not taking from each other but giving to each other what we really want, a love for each other's heart! In this, there is no conundrum only a fresh start through the heart.

A Love Life

My mind wanders too much
thinking of love lost
in a world thirsty for fear
while preferring the jeer.
I turn off my heart to the banter
of a fear infested recanter.
A moment of truth hypnotizes me
so full of love for the wrong things,
truelove escapes my mind,
but my heart can still sing
Love's melody.
Is this enough to find my lover?
I think not.
Presumably, I wonder and wander a lot
about the might it be, can it be,
or the what ifs and the why me
This is what rattles this way and that way
in my head
desiring to just sleep instead,
but never able to time out
that endless nothing in my head.
My heart flowing over with love,
but nothing motivates me to my feet
just this dread of ultimate defeat.
Retreat! Exclaims my nature,
while my heart argues with my mind
in a foreign language I did not know I had.
True Love has its own language
and while foreign to most,

one thing is obviously clear
it does not lie, cheat or steal.
A dying native language
being stolen on the lamb
but there is still hope
for those refusing in becoming
someone's dope on a rope.
I prefer to hope,
but I'm stuck in the muck of sin
waiting to be saved from drowning
in the depth of unfair,
and the deepest apologies
for a life gone wrong.
Angels farming to save my soul
can only produce fruit
if the seedling suckles
the attributes of a LOVE life
to serve, and love others.

Alone Together

A star lit night
wandering together in Franklin's Square
unaware of our future,
but deeply in love with the experience
of the here and now.
Wandering and strolling amidst quotes
of a life,
long lost in time,
but still as provoking to the mind,
and at times,
the heart.
I can't get you out of my head,
the things that were said
in a moment of unvarnished truth
or just a drunken stupor
full of pain for a desired love I can't ever have?!
Fate would agree with the latter,
the rest is just wishful chatter.
But this one moment frozen in memory
as infamous words from a glorious life
excited the mind.
Oh, what a time!
Two souls connected by a forbidden love,
spend time alone basking in the moonlight
with the stars leading the way
to a profound connection between two hearts.
Consuming the night in love,
alone and unafraid,
together but alone once again.

Amor a la Primera Vista

mi respiración se acelera
mi corazón corre
lágrimas de alegría
en mi alma lloré
por saber que mí amoroso
es único
y mío
el regalo del amoroso
y cariñoso

susurrando a mí corazón
el amor que siente por mí
sin embargo, la vergüenza
llenando el buzón de mí alma
con la sonrisa
que veo en los ojos
que nunca lo vi en otros
desconocidos

sobrevivimos juntos en un amor
lindo y especial
conociendo mí admirador
y aceptando que compartimos
uno con otro
el amor recibido
solo porque lo sentimos

no entendiendo porque
pero conozco
que es más espiritual que sexual
porque existe sin querer tocar

cuando los vimos por la primera vez
una energía de sostenimiento
que no fue nada de este mundo
pero algo más donde solo existe uno
feliz
encapsulado
en la fragancia dulce del amor
nada más me falta
ni tener que respirar

cuando se encuentra este amor
no te resistas por no entenderlo
porque la resistencia es puro dolor
no cómodo cuál dice el mundo
es puro locura
para tu futuro

amor a la primera vista
sí exista
solo si está abierto tu corazón
a recibirlo
sin vacilar
en la esperanza
del amor y corazón
acéptalo y ve
que este amor
es más, de conocerlos
es sobrevivir
en un mundo lleno
de los perdidos

Awake or Asleep

Love awakens to a new day,
and tells the world "Be happy today."
But most miss Love's message
because they sleep during this blessing.
Some receive it but become dismissing,
while others, presage the hate coming,
fall back to their slumbered sleeping.
A great blessing for receiving hearts,
accepting Love's announcement,
and dedicated to its pronouncement!
They feel the love that starts this day,
while others, asleep, get led astray.
Remaining open to satan's sensual decay.
Those awake, receive this Heavenly song
with the Celestial orchestrated throng,
singing Love's enchanting prolong.
Open your hearts to God's Love,
because this is your only saving grace.
The Bread of Life which saved truelove.
Wide awake, Love embraces,
and kisses your face.
Filling your heart with Love's grace
while evil easily erases.
So, awaken my love, to Love's awakening,
receiving this dawning
of His eternal blessing
while caressing and fawning
over Love's mysterious adorning.

LOVE

On this morning,
listen for Love's blessing,
and rejoice that you were not sleeping
or compromised by extravagant sinning!
Let Love caress your heart
at the dawn's early start,
so that you can melt a very cold heart.

Be Free

be free
    love somebody
        give freely
            be a true devotee
                love God immensely
            love your neighbor boldly
        you will then see
    how joyful you will be
for eternity

Be Love's Superstar

You are here today in a magnificent way!
Created and born as a blessing to others,
not so that you can squander it away
arguing and fighting with your mother,
with your brother, sister, and father,
and all those others.
Live up to the call of a greater day
by falling in love with love-to-love others.
Always be ready to bless a mess in trouble
because someone did it for you when you went astray.
Love does not judge or hold a grudge
love loves love for love of love,
and love makes it simple to indulge
in love's love for all every day.
Do this with all love's strength and power,
to love love for love's sake yesterday, today and tomorrow.
Live in love, because without it,
all you do is borrow it
while living a life full of horror,
where you can't believe in a hopeful tomorrow.
Be thoughtful and kind
because love will not bind you to time,
it frees your heart to expand your mind,
away from the unkind,
and rather to one of being inclined
to partake of Love's loving heart every single time
including this, and the next time
that someone is unkind.

Maybe then you won't go losing your mind.
Just remember this,
be Love's superstar next time.

Begging for Love

Please, I beg of you
My brothers and my sisters too
Love one another, for I know this to be true
God loves each one of you
It is not He who makes you blue
What the satan says to you is the untrue
This is who is behind your sadness
Do not pay no mind to his madness
He may dress it up like kindness
But deceit is his only brashness
Let your heart run to love
For this is our manna from above
Make your ways as gentle as a dove
And change your life to one of love!

Breaking Free in Quarantine

Another day in quarantine I scream,
the real kind that exists in my mind.
This is what people abhor,
not the physical chore
of staying inside.
No matter what, I cannot hide from me.
Will I muster the courage to forage
through the cobweb of clutter in me?
Can I pay the painful toll?
And what is my ultimate goal?
Instead, I keep busy going to and fro,
ignoring what is at my core,
but you reach a moment you can't ignore
those demons anymore.
We all have them, can't brag you don't,
that in itself, is just one more.
More frightening than any scary show
because you know the main character,
you're also intimate with the main plot;
that anchor to your soul.
It hits you like a well-placed punch,
but your hunch of what you fear
is not as bad as you thought.
When you cross to that other side.
you must first dance with your demon once more
like you did in the beginning.
Like you did when it came in through your front door
with hardly a startle.

Except this time, you will lead this dance,
taking a stance that this is no romance.
It's more like a fight,
but he knows your limited might and fright
in this complicated waltz.
It is necessary for your freedom to dive into this rabbit's hole without a tether.
It's the only way to sever from his endeavor to steal you forever.
Ignoring this dance while quarantined
you become filled with reluctance,
to embrace one another,
you and your self.
Can't just put it back on the shelf,
we don't know how long this will last.
Where can you go to escape?!
This exists inside you,
but so does the power to discover
that you can recover
with the help of another,
the source of all power.
First thing to do is about you
and not those quarantined with you,
stop using that excuse.
They can give you that moment to accept this dance,
not like they don't have other things they can do,
if they value you.
You're the reason they have an all access pass
to disturb and harass you.
You did this only to procrastinate
the waltz that needs to take place.
This is the real quarantine,
the one which exists in your heart and mind
and it can be quite unkind
if you choose to remain blind.

It will destroy your spirit
if you don't draw near it,
spin it
and give it a good unwind.
Breaking that bind
it has on your mind.
The only weapon or move you need?
The desire to succeed
and love indeed
but not just the love tied to human need.
Only agape love can break up this dance!

By Way of Forgiveness

Reeling from the demands of love and peace enmity,
I stumble, react and lash out to appease my enemy.
My love is choked off by grief in this lapse of honesty,
and the lies of dishonesty start filling my head with doubt and complacency.
I almost believe that I am lost,
never able to find my way home
to the place where love unfolds
the complexities of life.
While living in the snare of despair
I shout out to the hope that permeates the air which surrounds me,
"I need some direction!"
It takes effort on my part to wait and listen,
while I open my heart to catch it all.
Love responds on its own time
as it waits to assess my sincerity and ability to hear
with my heart.
When my mind steps out of the way,
I hear what love has to say,
"Love is faith, love, and charity
It can only walk in by the way of forgiveness.
You must leave your place of weakness and distress."

Dear Departed

With each passing of a loved one from this world it gets a little lonelier here. At first your numb and bellowing the fear of your loved one not being so near.

Next swaggers up guilt with a heap of jeer together with its piercing sneer, saying you had the chance to make a difference my dear.

If only this pain of the mundane was visible to my ear when they were here and so near. I could see to hear with my very own heart the weeping of my lonely heart once their light was blown out! If only I could listen to my site and ignite the fright before their flight into the night!

Daylight comes to save their memory from the delight of our fear that was nonexistent here when they were near. We grab on to every memory of delight and they agree it was not lonely for them because "you were my glee while I was near to thee. You made this world special to me when I was here and near."

Even as we grow another year without you here, I remember your joyful smile, your warm embrace, the heartfelt I love you that I once knew when you were here and near to me my dear.

I will embrace that you are here with me today, just in a different way. You caress my heart as I peer into that dark void of life and joy where you once stood here and near.

It is through this tear that I hear your love through this fondling of my heart. I am always near you my dear so do not fear for what was lost, which to both of us was very dear.

Desiring a New Start

Addiction is my fornication with death,
something always dies from it.
Love, memories, empathy,
relationships and honesty
as I develop this bad habit.
My vice becomes the answer to it all,
it satisfies my time awake,
and dulls the pain so I can sleep
or die to me in a panic.
Either way, I get some relief
from living in my lie.
Once a bright star,
I am now ignored
even from me.
Death, who recognizes my worry
keeps calling my name,
and beckoning me to share in his game.
Healing is as near as my heart,
but as long as I think
that I'm smarter than smart,
healing is a train
that barrels past that station
of my heart.
It cannot stop on its own,
it must be stopped by Love
desiring a new start.

¿Despierto o Dormido?

En la mañana se despierta el Amor,
despierto le dice al mundo,
"No tengas ningún rencor."
Pero no todo el mundo lo escucho
por estar dormidos en cuando habló,
el sol de Amor.
Que lastima y dolor
que no sé haya escuchado el anunció.
El Amor despierto y atento
por todos que buscan el alimento,
que Dios único nos dio.
El pan de vida y amor
que sostiene el alma de uno.
Para unos solo por el momento.
Por otros, muy lento el refresco,
se vuelve al dormido.
Por el que lo recibió y guardo el anuncio
recibe el abrazo y beso
del Amor siempre despierto
y atento al corazón.
Despierto y escuchando
el anuncio del Amor
también escuchando la música
celestiales del Amor
Todopoderoso.

Do It for Love

What is on your mind?
More of the unkind?
Let us hit the rewind.

Imagine this: An eternal bliss.
What will it consist?
I can assure you it is no evil hiss,
no culture of dismiss
or full of protracted excuses,
my dearest.

No blatant lie,
No wanton rely
on the needy I.
We should start today
this day
to get far away
from this evil foray.

A head start
for all who are smart.

Love with love to love
whomever God said to love.
Love is Truth,
Truth is Love
When you see a dove from above
do you perceive it as uncouth, my love?
Do you use it as a ruse for you to lie thereof?

The Truth is obvious
unless you think lying is religious
then you go about the frivolous,
believing in the ridiculous.

God set His Spirit free
to scour the earth for you and me,
for all those souls wanting to be free,
receiving the truth from the living tree.
He calls you and me
to invite Love into your heart
and let this Truth be,
to be the head start
to sanctify thee.

For Heaven's sake,
do this for Love's sake.
Otherwise,
this will be our greatest mistake.

Do You Really Love Me?

God asks, do you love me?
Yes, I do.
Do you really love me?
Yes, I do.
Do you love me?
You know I do.
Have you fed my lambs?
Is that what I'm to do?
Have you cared for my sheep?
Is that what I'm to do?
Have you fed my sheep?
Is that what I'm to do?
You must follow me.
What about that one behind me?
Why are you worried about others?
Oh, I'm just supposed to follow?
I've taught and told you what I require of you.
This happens as a habit
because we lack attention to read the Word
much less grab it,
and never let it go.
We like to read it and forget it,
thinking it very circumspect.
So we disrespect,
but God does not forget
and then we are filled with all this regret.
I bet you think and fret
about the time
you did not forgive that debt.

Or at least I hope you do.
What are we to do?
Exactly what you know to be true!
Be merciful, love justice
and walk humbly with God.
Is this what I'm to do?
Generation after generation
Round robin, round robin
We just keep robbing our soul of its true goal.
Love to love and love again
until your love loves love
for being so.

El Silencio Despierta Tu Amor

Tranquilo en el oscuro alrededor,
iluminando mí espíritu
y cuidando mí corazón.
Rezando para la paz del mundo
y para mí absolución.
Qué lindo es el silencio,
tremendo y cariñoso
con el amor que me regaló mí Diosito,
El Santísimo Jesucristo
y El Espíritu Santo.
La Trinidad santísima
para hoy, mañana y eternidad.
No hay ninguna razón
de tener miedo del oscuro alrededor
y el silencio que magnífica tu corazón,
encontrándose
con el Amor.

Grief Stricken

A love loss is happening right now, wandering alone is commonplace until you reach a loving home. A home where love roams freely, where you feel loved. When darkness comes from nowhere there is a scare when you think 'I'm all alone somehow!' There is a loud groan when you roam alone until you reach that home, that special home, which makes you feel not alone. We live our waking moments looking and waiting for those precious moments, those tender words, only to spend those lonely moments all alone when darkness comes unexpectedly. No one knows my loneliness, we share it alone, that hurtful groan with being alone and no one really knowing how to console my breaking heart. We try to console but does that lonely heart know that they are loved by someone, and everyone when they hurt all on their own? Does it matter when you are alone in the darkness feeling the numbness of loneliness? It matters to me that I can see a soul in trouble and their spirit is broken but can I comfort that lonely heart? Can I walk with that lonely soul and do my part? Maybe in matters like these it is best to see the heart as a doorway. A doorway that passes through death to life crying out I love you; I love you; I love you, throughout.

Hide and Seek

What am I looking for?
Do I really know?
Is it love, or the I told you so?
Am I looking for shame?
Fame?
A sex game?
More of the boring insane?
What am I looking for?
Love, in all the wrong places?
Well, where are all the right damn places?
Do you know?!
If so, why don't you share the info?
Keeping it for yourself?
Well, that's mighty greedy
when you know there are so many needy.
What am I looking for?
Happiness and joy?
Oh boy, what does this employ?
Money or pride?
I just want to hide,
but then I'm just looking
for shadows in the dark.
What am I looking for?
Surely, it's not anything I will find in this world
that will complete me.
I've tried them all.
What am I looking for?
I get it! I am looking for me!
Why am I chasing me all around?

Why am I playing hide and seek with myself?
I am getting lost inside of me,
no wonder no one can help me!
I'm playing tag with myself looking for help.
What am I looking for?
I am looking for help!
From someone other than me,
but I have to say something out loud and make my decree,
or I turn to God like Jesus said.
What am I looking for?
Maybe I'm not meant to know me.
Maybe I'm just supposed to trust the love inside of me.
Maybe I'm supposed to act
and not overthink this fact.
Maybe I should trust
that love will lead me
in the right path for me
and reveal things of glee
as I grow in love with thee.
What am I looking for?
Love, for you and me.

Hope

What is your great hope?
That today turns into tomorrow?
That yesterday lives in today?

What is your great hope?
That your worth is worthless?
That you are the great hope?

What is your great hope?
That we can restore the planet to its previous glory?
That every human life is cherished?

What is your great hope?
That all hunger can be fed?
That all can drink clean water?

What is your great hope?
That the homeless find a home?
That the naked can be clothed?

What is your great hope?
That peace between people is attainable?
That peace between societies can be achieved?

What is your great hope?
That violence disappears?
That lust is quenched by chastity?

What is your great hope?
That you have a job?
That you can afford your life?

What is your great hope?
That someone wipes away your tear?
That someone makes you smile?

What is your great hope?
Love
Where is your great hope?
Love
Why is there great hope?
God is love

What is hopeless?
Having to ask this question
when you lack forgiveness.

Hypocrisy Destroyed Love

A gem, a treasure.
A pleasure to be around.
Their voice, a pleasant sound.
A loving embrace, such a gentle creature,
starts the race on love's merry-go-round.
Their love in full view, they abound
in romantic ecstasy.
Then enters hypocrisy,
crashing these feelings to the ground.
I love you my way intimately,
I love you your preferred way intensely.
The two, profound,
always looking for the way around,
and mistake our love willingly
while giving it to another one in town.
We both frown.
We both want to wear the crown
and we forego intimacy.
What happened to the love we once knew?
One kidnapped the others' view
and threw it out the window,
a blow to the others' ego.
Two acting like one,
then the one acting like two
again, and again,
until feelings begin to wane.

We forgot how to love each other,
and now only tolerate the other in vain.
With nothing left to gain,
we attempt to explain
a way out.
Never to be quite the same again.

I Love You!

I cannot deny that I love you.
I never want to be apart
because your smile caresses my heart.
I start to realize that I must be
a better me as a gift to you
so that I please your heart
just as you do for me.
This is the least that I could do
in exchange for your love.
My purpose is clear,
it is to love you like no other my dear.
To hold you and make you laugh.
To hold you when you are sad.
To give you my heart,
if that is what you ask for,
because without you,
what would I need it for?
When we must part,
I keep you in my heart
and remember all the things about you,
so I can feel close to you.
The warmth of your smile,
the way the sun shines off your hair,
your loving eyes beckoning me closer,
it is no big surprise
that I get lost in the dream of your scent,
your scent left behind on my mind,
when we embraced for the first time.
The feeling of not wanting to let you go.

I could have stayed in your embrace forever
and let the world go on with its crazy race.
I found my place, right here with you.
A beautiful oasis.
Love, happiness, joy and hope
all coming together for the first time,
in a stranger, but for the first time
because it is our time.
Love like this only happens once
because duplicates and repeats are but a trance
which is only looking for this one ultimate romance.
We exist in our love for each other.
Today is the first day of the rest of my life,
because your heart tells mine that this is so.
When your heart kissed mine,
it ignited a flame of joy and an eternal smile
that would walk a mile
just to fetch your favorite candy
because your sweetness
is what I craved to give me a purpose.
It is only the time apart that brings sorrow to my heart,
but I know that we carry each other's love
tucked safely in a safe place
because it is more precious than gold.
Like the sun's warm kiss,
so your love is to my existence.
Your love makes me grow
only to love you even more each day
in a way that the Heavenly Angels sing about love.
Because words fail
to really capture what I really want to say,
I must settle for nothing better than
I love you
yesterday, today, and tomorrow.

Pay no attention to the sorrow
of our existing apart
because I will always carry you in my heart
until that day
that we will be together
forever in one heart.

In Love for Love with Love

I think I have lost my mind.
Oh, wouldn't that be so fine?
The excuse of a lifetime,
especially because I'm speaking of what's unkind.
Things that blow one's mind
trying to figure out if I'm God aligned,
or inclined to malign mankind.
One thing is true is my heart and mind,
a contempt for the lying mastermind.
Remember Jesus said that a house divided will fall?
So, what does it benefit the devil to have me on call?
On call to promote love?
You do see how that would not be a very smart move on his part,
getting you to think with your heart.
Writing about what is tearing us apart.
Which way should you think?
The Truth or the doublethink?
Does is hurt your head to bethink
that which you must rethink?
While you accept the love implication,
but dismiss the devil & demons' fornication.
Such s verbal aberration.
Does this cause you a spiritual agitation?
Get over your courteous fury bola
and go read St. Ignatius of Loyola
or the prophets Elijah and Jeremiah.
All saying God has told you.
You dare ask, told me what?

let's start with this part
are you able to distinguish the two apart?
The mind and the heart.
What about that which is tearing down your ideological rampart?
It's ok, God will rebuild you in love to start,
but you must obey and be stalwart.
Beckon the Holy Spirit to enter your heart
to love for love with love.

La Voz de Amor

El medio ambiente habla del amor,
el aire me toca el corazón
con dulce palabras del cariño
lo escuchó mí alma.
¿Para qué me busca?
Porque estoy perdido
y no entiendo de este dolor.
¿Qué quieres saber del amor?
¿De dónde vienes
y pará dónde vas?
¿Me explicas tus secretos
en estos momentos?
Buscó el corazón humilde
porque esos saben
lo que es cariño
y el amor busca lo mismo.
¿Por qué, si es cariñoso,
duele mucho
cuando lo busco?
El dolor es parte del amor
para que sepas
que lo bonito cuesta mucho.
¿Con que pago el boleto
sí tanto así cuesta?
Lo puedes pagar
con una fiesta de sonrisas
o también con un alma de bella vistas.
¿Y si te buscó y no estás allí?
Siempre estoy aquí, atrás y allá.

No me tiene que buscar por mucho
porque andaré en tú lado
cargándote si es necesario.
¿Cuándo sé que eres tú?
Cuando sientes el aire de placer
y te cuento en poema
el amor y cariño
que es necesario saberlo,
para vivir una vida entera
y próspera.
Ésa es la voz y presencia del amor.

Live in Love

Another year in the past,
A new year rushing in fast
At last, I know what I'm looking for
Love, forevermore!
Let me loose from all your lies,
You wannabe, buzzing around like flies.
You scheme and pretend
But no one believes or can comprehend
The evil nature of your sin
All you desire is the win!
You are what is wrong with this world
And own real estate in the netherworld.
You say $1+1=27\times5\div92$ and such
Just hush already, you are a bit too much.
You live in your own mind
While your spirit is genuinely unkind.
The art of the lie,
Requires me to comply.
To deny and forfeit,
Relying solely on silly wit.
Then I realize
I'm the prize
Everyone is fighting for!
Couldn't see it through the lies galore
I must learn to live in love
And take my orders from Above!

Llegó el Amor

El amor llega como luz brillante
solo para decir que despierta
mi amor elegante.
Llegó el amor por la ventana,
de esperanza y cariño,
qué lástima que unos no aguanta
y se conforma con un amor pequeño.
Te amo, dice el aire,
y el sol le acompaño
con un abrazo cariñoso y amoroso.
Dulce palabras dicho en voz bajo
porque el amor puro
no debe de ser duro u oscuro
ni por gritando que no está seguro.
Alegría lo guía por siempre
y nos regocijamos
del amor que aprende
cómo amarse uno con otros y no ser tontos.
Será una vida muy triste
si no existe este tipo de amor
en tu corazón.
Abierto y aceptando
el amor del corazón
deja el mundo
sin moretón
y dejándonos lleno del amor.

Love Forevermore

Love can help you heal
      without it you may lie cheat or steal
Love is blind to hate and will reduce your anger
      offering hope and making you stronger
Love, love, love forevermore
      and hope for what's in store
Love, love, love
      forevermore!

Love is Brand New

I stand at the top of a mountain, feeling the air move around me while the sun pierces my skin and warms my soul. I am washed over with love and joy.

Abruptly the wind whips up and I stumble; dark and menacing clouds obstructs the sun's healing glow and it suddenly becomes cold, the chill in the wind stings my skin. I feel my life is suddenly in danger again.

I begin to wonder about my life and I easily forget that just a moment ago I was in love and a joyful delight.

Danger rears its dangerous spirit and drawing myself ever closer to be near it I allow it to take over my soul, and reluctant or too afraid to let it go.

Just as the web of a spider, so intricate and delicate, but needed for sustenance or quite the opposite; those web of lies we adapt to our lives; we compromise our security of Love's promise to keep us safe, secure or sure of God's promise.

Why is it in my nature to make love a compromise of lies and deceit instead of a retreat for finding the joy in a stranger's heart I meet on the street? For how can it really matter that I look for love in a heart I already know and love? What fruit will this gather?

My love has become really unkind; it is so selfish that I can no longer claim it to be love but some atrocious, attractive, and simple negotiable mime of mine trying to be kind, which is not love at all in anyone's mind.

As I sit on that mountain top, scared and alone while the wind whips around, making me cold to the bone, I shout to the heavens: "Shall I go it alone, am I on my own?"

A single drop of water falls from the sky and gently caresses my cheek, mingling with my tears of fear. It startles me but awakens in me a love so dear, one I never knew before. One of forgiveness, mercy, justice, and grace for the human race.

I realize in this turmoil of trouble that all this of being in a state of alone and afraid is just a charade of lies greater and more extravagant than a Mardi Gras parade.

That single tear from heaven washed away my fear and pain, and now I'm new again with a love that repairs the heart over and over, again and again.

A special love has filled my heart and this love is reserved for all of mankind, especially for those who are mean and unkind. Those who think love is but a chore to score points and to bore a rabbit hole for the soul to wander about in the dark and cold.

I am free to Love and feel joyful no matter what weather I gather on the top of that mountain of mine. Love is brand new, and I will never have to bid it adieu.

Love is true to me and to all of you.

Love is My Voice

When love is your center, your all,
there is this nurturing call.
A call that brings you home
to those loving warm arms
encircling you, and keeping you from harm.
It is a safe place,
and it fills the entire space
no more black hole
in your soul.
No more loneliness.
No more going it alone.
No more idleness
No more entitlements.
No more gluttonous mess.
You rise out of this state of staleness
into a beautiful awareness,
that love is your new home.
Hope and joy will you now roam.
So do not bemoan,
rejoice!
You have been given a new voice!
Beware the liar that tries to steal it,
just look up in love and God will heal it.
He will renew your spirit
so that love is what you inherit.

Love, what a devotion!
Greatest of all emotion,
a power all its own
and a freedom once unknown
before that glorious day
that Love made it possible for us to come home.

Love is Waiting in My Heart

Come into my heart my love,
I am waiting for you there.
Alone I get confused
about what I am supposed to do.
I forget to be kind
and only listen to my mind.
With you, my love, I am so different,
with you I am aware of my indifference.
Come into my heart my love,
I am waiting for you there.
Without you I misconstrue the truth,
I easily get distracted, acting uncouth.
I forget my place in this holy race,
a tarnished testament to my own faith.
Come into my heart my love,
I am waiting for you there.
I fall and cannot regain my composure,
without your love I'm just a poser.
An empty shell of wanting desire,
chasing every opportunity for an empire.
Come into my heart my love,
I am waiting for you there.
I make the mistake that you departed,
only because my mind is thwarted.
You live in my heart always and in all ways,
for in all ways, you love me always.
Come into my heart my love,
I am waiting for you there.

My love and your love mingle in my heart,
in every way we are one love, never apart.
This truth is as timeless as Truth,
as intimate as love itself, for it is Truth.
Come into my heart my love,
I am waiting for you there.
It is me that departs my own heart,
seeking something without a heart.
Seeking and searching without finding,
what is already waiting in my own heart.
Come into my heart my love,
I am waiting for you there.
This invitation is my own heart
screaming out to me from the start!
My love and your love are always one,
and never will I be a lonely one all alone.
In my heart together in love,
a blessing & grace from our Lord above!

Love, m'kay!

Love is like a cool autumn night after a sun-drenched day,
m'kay!
Love is like the last day of school with summer on the way,
m'kay!
Love is like sweet roasted corn drenched in butter or Parkay,
m'kay!
Love is like your first payday,
m'kay!
Love is like your first car and first trip away,
m'kay!
Love is like these but really its own doorway,
m'kay!
Love opens a world of peace, so don't delay,
m'kay!
If you lost your way today,
do not let hate have its way,
Love in earnest anyway,
Love is only a smile and a compliment away,
m'kay!

Love Whispers

My heart steals a glance,
I cannot look away.
Our stares lock on to each other
while our hearts start to dance.
From across the room
I can taste what makes you special.
My skin absorbs your energy,
and the beauty in your eyes
entices my advance.
Our hearts continue to dance.
All around us the world spins violently,
but time stands still
as we take each other into our hearts.
Slowly you peel away the layers
of hurt and shame
and we excite the game.
Never to be alone again,
no roaming the lonely.
Our love ignites and satisfies,
no more hopeless nights
and as I fight back my tears
you rush to kiss my cheek,
my neck, my lips.
Whispering "I Love you" in my ear
and eliminating all my fear.
Can I be candid my dear?
What brought you here?

With a grin and a wink,
you whisper my name
and we do it all over again.

Love's Caviar

My heart and mind awaken at first light.
The dawn of a new day,
    with it comes hope's delight
        and a desire for beautiful things to say!
This day I pray
    that God's might
        will take away all the fright
            and true love will ignite
                the passions of loving love's love
                and loving love alone
                so love's love
                can bring you home
                to love's loving abode
                where love calls His throne
                and where we are never alone!
Bright and early, filled with hope and love
    let not this feeling fade, my love!
Do not let someone steal love's parade.
Let your love comfort others today.
Be that bright and shiny star
    that lights the way, near and far,
        with love's caviar.
Inspirational and radiant hope
    which guides your way
        to love's loving embrace
            beyond the stars!

Love's Great Escape

I was walking through a sea of pain,
                the waves of hate crashed over me
again, and again
                                I could barely catch my breath.
            A whirlpool of misery opened up
and it swallowed me whole
                          I ended up in this black hole
                of despair
                I gasped for air.
                          Wishing You were there
                              to help me out
but I was all alone.
I tried to get away,
                I tried yelling and screaming
but only silence won my voice
                              terror and fear gripped my feet
I could not move.
                              I was standing and running
                in one direction.
I was lost in this place
                          a torment of race after race
in this nowhere place.
                Sad and lonely
                I cried myself to sleep awake.
This place makes no sense
                            pretentious parading around me
                while cowardice lifted me up
                            and fakeness cheers me on.
Cold while hot tears
dried up before they cascade.
                      I know in my heart that I must depart
                            or live here forever
                with my lost and confused.

I secretly plan my escape
        unbeknownst to my mind
                where it all started.
I invite love to find You.
      My heart is in charge
    giving me strength and courage
       the power of love
     encourages me to move on.
      Love's unmatched power
  led me to truth's lifesaving lifeline.
      The terrible chaos is over.
I was lurched out of the porridge of staleness,
  and I shine brightly in a new awareness,
      that something can be new,
   and that something is me and You!
      Love will get me through
   and bring me to a fabulous place
     where peace, joy, and hope
     share and absorb my pain.
       I start living again
 and my life will never be the same.
     I must rebuke the satan's
       scheme to be mean.
         I am new!
  Now let love live strong in me
       So that I can be
      the salt and light
    you wanted me to be!

Love's Great Roar

To ignore hate
    is to agitate
        the status quo
We can't sit this one out
    desiring only to pout
        while evil goes all out
We were not created to doubt
    we were meant to shout
        what love is all about
Tell me more
    tell me more
        of love's great roar
            God loves you
                forevermore!

Love's Warm Embrace

You feel a warm embrace and the Sun kisses your face.
Your lost in the ecstasy of the feeling that you have met your saving grace.
An understanding of time and space.
Everything coming together in your heart and you put on that happy face.
This time it is real, no make believes skipping around in outer space.
The warmth of love radiates, and motivates, and ends that hopeless chase.
The Sun kisses my face again and again, without any demands that I join a race.
No more races to nowhere races!
No more marathons of empty dark places!
I belong to the Sun that kissed my face and fills my heart with warm embraces.
No more walking around confused and forgotten in the dark places of my mind.
No more of the unkind!
Lifted up above the Angels in the high oasis of the Morning Light that kisses faces,
and brings you in for warm embraces.
I forget all about the bad and dark races to places of ill regard.
Instead, I find myself submitting to the free will of choosing happy and warm places.
Here in this love with nothing but happy faces,
greeting me with infinite kisses and warm embraces.
So happy to see me while ignoring my weaknesses of shame and waste.
Meekness and kindness exude and rejoices in this happy oasis of this warm place
where the Sun kisses your face and showers all with warm embraces.
You lose yourself in this place but not to confusion and darkness.
You lose yourself to the Sun kissing your face, and that warm embrace
that led you away from your dark and lonely place.

You have won your race!
Sitting on the mantel of mercy and grace,
while the Sun once again kisses your face and gives you that eternal embrace.
Love has carried you over to a sacred space
filled with Love which radiates brighter than the sun we know.
A place where we shine and glow because the Son, "I am," kisses your face
and welcomes you with the warmest embrace!

Maybe We Can Do Better

My frequent dismay of this horrible display of hate and intolerance for our fellow sojourner is by and large tempered by the way we aspire to foray into a season of love so profound that it can only be found in God, the Son, and the Holy Spirit. To hear it makes me want to be completely immersed in it! There are so many evils in the world all dolled up in glam and glitz that we are tempted by their beauty to accept the lie within it. Never to realize I've been misled until Truth and Love pull out that thread that lead it to unravel revealing the lie contained within that fake beauty that drew us near it. We are all guilty of it, this wondering and wandering spirit of guess what's in it. Ever looking for that next thrill or big shrill of temporary satisfaction that comes with that tempting infraction of common decency and protraction of the inaction to love. Maybe we can do better, be better, expect better, choose better, die better, forgive better, live better, suffer better, cry better, feel better, pray better, relax better, compromise better, give better, love better. Maybe we should hope for better than what we deserve since love, and this is true, can forgive a multitude of sin.

Ministry of Love

I worked miracles for you to believe,
but you doubted and took your leave.
Can you love Me?
I healed the sick for you to believe,
you accused me of trying to deceive.
Can you trust Me?
I expelled demons for you to believe.
You said it was from the demons, and you disbelieve.
Can you believe Me?
I raised dead to life for you to believe me,
but you still grieve.
Can you place your hope in Me?
All I did was for you to believe in Me,
but you still doubt God's reprieve.
Can you surrender your pride to Me?
The Holy Spirit, sent for you to believe,
continues My ministry of undeceive.
Can you obey me?

Will you join me?

Journey with Me into true Love!

My Heart Beats Again

I opened my eyes like any other day,
but this day was the start of a new life.
I knew what I knew yesterday
they were cutting me open with a knife.
My heart struggled to beat,
not enough of life's blood would arrive
in time to repeat
those beats that makes life thrive.
I can feel every beat drumming aloud
and I feel every thump like never before
filling up the room where death is allowed
but not this day, a day I can adore.
God, by His action, said you're not done
so, I start living a new life of love
no more of that dismissive pun
that I cannot join those living above.
It is my time to live in love
to be loved, and to love Love all over again,
because I've learned that love cannot be undone.
A rallying cry of rejoice!
For every person that lives in love
inherits a beautiful voice.
Blessings delivered by the Dove
from Heaven above.
So, rejoice,
and fall in Love!

My Mother

There will never be a word
That would ever suit my Mother.
There is no feeling that equals
Her Love for me,
In fact there is no touch either,
Nothing can replace her embrace
Not even on God's green earth.
Because my Mother was made
Just for me,
And me for Her
Because we were meant to be
Together, forever.
It is to my advantage
That I always recall
That without Mom,
I would be no one.
Because I was growing inside
For as long as it took,
To make sure that I became somebody.
Then came the after
Which I reckon,
Caused a headache or two.
Maybe even three, four, or even more.
Or what about that time
I was so rude?
But Mother knew best
So she just let me stew,
She knew,
I had a lot of growing yet to do.

Why even when she was angry
I probably did not help matters
Especially when I made Her cry.
The only thing she held onto,
The only thing she knew
Was that we were meant to be together,
since the first time she felt me move.
Mom is my connection to this world
And the world that I come from,
One of love and affection.
My Mom made sure I was safe.
To make it all this way
She took care of me when I was a baby,
And even when I was fifty.
A smile, a kiss, even a loving glance.
Remembering when
she first laid eyes on me.
I asked Her once,
Was I a good baby?
Did I ever make you angry?
She looked at me with love and a smile,
Why you were nothing but a joy to me.
Her Love overtakes my mistakes
Because she was my shelter
Before I entered the world
We all run after.
But my real home
Was always with Her,
The very moment
I started growing inside Her.
Now I know this to be true,
That my Mother and me
We're meant to be together.

Nothing could be truer
Than somebody coming to life
Inside of you.
Connected by love
Our relationship
Grew and grew.
Let me introduce you
To my Mother,
Madrecita Madre, esplendidez,
Guadalupe Ramon
Hernandez

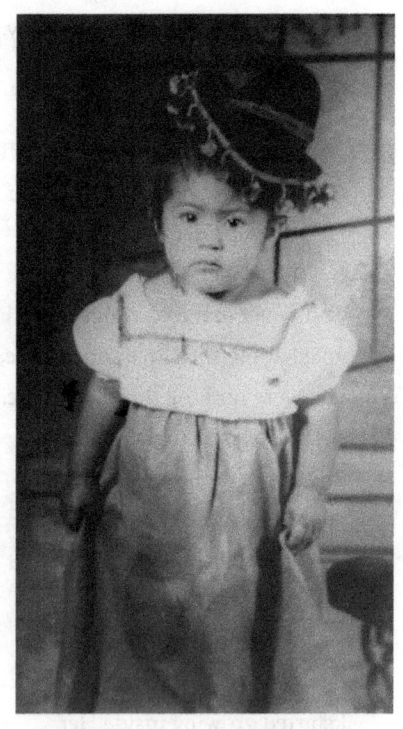

My One-Time, One-of-a-Kind

Has this world always been so noisy?
Besides all this yelling and screaming
you have all this commentary streaming.
More like people just being nosy
with them constantly complaining
about a better life being more rosy.
While wasting their lives masturbating
their minds.
A world turned cold on the sexy grinds,
and now even sexuality is about debating the several kinds.
Becoming so fixated on stimulation
we stroke and absorb all this self-admiration.
Taking endless shots of self-adulation
until we're broke from all this pent-up frustration.
We invent a new workstation
mining for idle speculation.
Shoveling greed down our throats
posting and posting our social posts.
We can't get enough of the hateful jokes.
While we dance in flames of backstrokes,
from regret to guilt to an intentional hoax.
Fighting for a peaceful life
while kicking and punching
the heart of life.
Believing we are prone to all this strife
living inside the walls of a self-righteous wife.
Fear is ticking,
like a bomb ready to take away our life.

Love

Tick-tock, tick-tock
you are racing against the clock,
with no idea of where to dock.
Steering right past that bedrock
that could stop the ticking of that clock,
but too focused on that Glock
you're aiming at your head
loaded with any roadblock.
Self-inflicted wounds become paramount
while loving ourselves, we place this on a discount.
Letting our loathing surmount,
always searching for an ugly way to dismount.
This is no life for the living,
the absence of all thanksgiving.
Were you only able to see and feel,
the love inside you?
Your true appeal!
What do I see and feel in your misdirected zeal?
You are a one-time, one-of-a-kind,
too beautiful to become a mime
and too true to live in a bind of the stand-behind.
I will wrestle with the satan to win your mind,
and love you like the angels to expose the sublime
of the true you in this time.
Just let me be near you
and let our hearts speak the truth to each other
while we console one another
in matters of love, passion, and the honesty
I stole to enter your heart.
I love you more than the art of your mess up,
or whatever ill will you hold to be true
in all your negative pileup.
My love is deep and strong
ready and excited to take your heart on,
and fill you with the warmth of the Son.

For it is only by His love that I can take you on.
I promise that if you let our hearts mingle
in this ocean of love, you will not become undone.
You will be in peace
and joyful in knowing that real love
is truthful and hopeful.
You will soon realize
that your new life has begun.
I love you dearly
My one time,
one-of-a-kind!

Ode to the Bygone Days

Back to normal is the battle cry,
gotta want to win the war and not defy.
Practice safety for all of us
not only the me, myself and I.
Believing in things that only mystify.
All these lies that are superfluous.
Normal?! Lot's wife did defy,
longing for the past to gratify
her demise seemingly pernicious.
God wants to save and beautify,
expecting us to trust and edify
not engage in actions treasonous.
Trust in the Lord most high,
with His heavenly throne in the sky,
believe in God's plan and love for us!

Peek a Boo

Peek-a-boo
                                  To all of you
and imagine all your dreams came true
                                  What would you wish for? Do you have a clue?
What would this world do?
                                  Pursue love or wish it adieu?
It's your wish so search your heart,
                                  Will love reign or would you demand it to part?
Don't be such a worrywart,

Create a world of love and create true art!

The Mastermind of Love

Do you mind if I embellish in rhyme?
I must get something off my mind,
It goes to this thing called a love crime.
Many believe we are intertwined,
Others of the notion of the self-sublime.
Who can lead me to the true find?
You must start at the beginning of time,
Where there existed no lie of any kind.
Then pride and disobedience align,
God's perfect love distorted by mankind.
God's mercy is true, our mistake, benign,
But it must take a Holy One of a Kind!
He will bring only one sign,
A message from the Mastermind
Love is not the crime,
It is what each of you must find.
A true test of time,
Love, and be kind.

The Uncle You Can Forget

I'm the uncle you can forget
I am not trying
    to be your friend
        for what I say
            does not follow any trend
                of the ancient demon
                    of offend,
for I know one day
    you will regret that bet.
What I share is but a dare
    to stare
        into your soul
            with eyes wide open
                and be aware!
In times of trouble
    who will wobble
        and who will steer you
            out of trouble?!

The Steady Hand of Love

There is an ocean so deep
that to look into it,
you see the sea.

To the beholder of this vision
it can terrify your ability to conceive
such a confusion.

The turmoil of waves crashing on waves
and pounding on other waves.
Whirlpools opening within whirlpools.
The water deep and dark as the night
without the moonlight
glistening on it's might.

The thunderous screams
of violent turmoil
causing you fright.
They beckon you to jump into this night.
This liquid night of the deep.
Plentiful delights of anguish,
and violent energy
to stimulate your sleepy tranquility.

What is this sea under the ocean saying to me?
Why do I feel the urge to jump
into this deep confusion
that lacks any sincerity?

Am I excited
by that violent turbulence of energy
because I have become dull?
Or is it me feeling comfort in the draw?
Only to scream for help
when I jump into it all.

There is but one hand
that will draw you out
of this deep and dark abyss,
or keep you from jumping into this fall.

The steady hand of Love
is the only sure assist
to protect you from it all!

Toxic Love

Clowns and Jesters
doing what they do best,
silly meddling of my love again.

Or is it really the other way around?
Have I been the clown,
disrupting your playground?

Am I entertaining my pride and ego,
while I listen to you cry?

Did I forget the pain so soon,
of that time you stood over me?
While I cried in tune
with the misfortune
you conceived for me?

We are so cruel to each other
but desire one another
like an addict with his vice
needing that fix like good advice.

Trying to be nice to each other
but only while in paradise
otherwise,
we compromise.

Depending on how bad we have it
we compel love to take a hike
only to ignite the fright
of losing each other.

Pushing ourselves away,
far far away,
and exclaim
atop a mountain of fake cheers,
our imaginary love.

You and I both know
we can walk
whenever we choose.
Like death, we all walk alone.

The only exemption is redemption
and a new kind of love
one that evolution cannot control.

One that is bold in love
and home to the true Holy Spirit.

Welcome to Love

Am I or am I not me,
    in these times of I can't think on my own
        but fooled to think I do,
            I really don't know what to think.
I know I feel like me
    but this could be me deceiving me
        and I am really not me.
Staring into the mirror I see
    what appears to be a reflection of me
        or at least someone who appears
            to be me.
Hey! Who are you? Speak to me
    but there is only a cold stare,
        unaware of what to say.
People call me by what I think is my name,
    but this could all be a game
        because I think I would have
            a bit more fame
                not this lame version of who I think I am.
If I were me, I would be,
    someone other than me,
        because I know what I know
            and that is so much more
                that could have bought me more
                    in this life I think might be mine.

LOVE

Fantastical delusions from my mind
    only bind me to ridiculous skepticisms,
        because how could I not be me
            if I see me all the time
                and I have to live with me?
Knowing me all my life
    should make this easy
        that I must be the very me I lost
            somewhere along the way of life.
How could this have happened?
That I have become such a skeptic
    that I can even question
        who it is to be me.
You silly little rabbit
    tricks are for the lost and stolen
        not for those who live by love alone.
Only if the hope of love is broken
    can you believe other's
        broken lies and their strides
            to recruit you into the world of demise.
A world reserved for the never time.
Awaken your heart to love
    and get to know the real you
        created to smile, hope, and live in love.
Rejoice with your new voice
    and rebuke all liars and desires
        to strip the love from you and others.
Welcome to love, the love that was gifted from above.

Win My Heart

The electric tingling from my lover's caress jump starts my heart,
It makes my heart explode with joy and laughter.
I don't want this moment to end.
I delay the good-byes
with one more kiss
time stands still, and I win Love's promise.
Love's promise to not pretend.
Unable to focus, my mind wanders around in my heart,
love stricken and no inkling of what is normal
because I have received a fresh start.
Fresh and new like the morning dew
I drink it all in, and share it with my lover,
under the cover of love and affection.
Sheer satisfaction!
My knees become weak
as I seek the source of love in my lover's eyes
while I lose control of my senses
that are now under my lover's control.
How bold!
Take control of me my love
lead me to a love beaming with
affection and satisfaction
gifted from above
and seen in the reflection of my lover's stare.
Staring into my soul and filling me with the ecstasy of Love's true goal.
To win my heart for one more day.

Light

The first Words from God were let there be Light, in the beginning of Creation. Fast forward to Jesus, the Word made flesh, and He says that He is the light of the world and that all who follow Him will not walk in darkness but have the light of life. He instructs us to let our light shine before people so that they can give honor to our Father in heaven. So, what is this light? Does it radiate or does it illuminate? I will let you decide.

When I was a young child, I was aware of God's existence because of my parent's devotion, through my religion but most importantly it was through faith that I believed in God. I was too young in faith and in knowledge to experience God. Even in prayer, I had this understanding that God exists but only by worldly experience. In a way, you can say that I was in darkness. From a toddler until I reached the age of ten, I have no recollection of ever experiencing God's light and was occupied with childish things, as any average child would be. I went to school, I played games with my brother and our friends outside. I watched one of three channels on TV with my family. I went to Church and Sunday school. One of my fondest memories of childhood was rushing to take my father's work boots off when he arrived home from work. I had no experience of spiritual enlightenment but only recognized light as the world understands it. I turned a light switch on and there was light. I lit a candle, and it provided a soft and relaxing light. I used a flashlight to get around in the dark, or I lit a lantern when power went out during a Southeast Texas thunderstorm to illuminate the darkness around me or to read my comics.

It was much later in life, after I had my first experience with God that I was reborn in the Spirit and started walking in the light of life because I made a conscience effort to follow Jesus. I picked up my cross with love and chose to be obedient to God's will. This brings an illumination of one's Spirit, an understanding, an enlightened consciousness of a life lived to glorify God. This type of light is only attained through a desire to have an intimate relationship with God, and it is through this love that light becomes more than just an illuminating factor, it becomes a state of existence in the light of God. You are invited into this light, to come into existence in the very light of God where you receive truth and love. As you grow spiritually in the light, it reveals those things of the Spirit that you could not see (experience) before. Your understanding is elevated to receive profound revelations through your personal experience of God. You are moved to actions and charity that desire to glorify God with no expectations for a reward, and you are compelled to honor God. To love God, to please God, to worship God, to serve God, to converse with God, to be intimate with God and to serve others with the same love and excitement. It is at this time that you radiate God's love outward, and you become the light in a dark world. Illuminating and radiating.

God's Light is so bright that nothing can extinguish its might!

A Christian

A ll this positivity
C an be disturbing to some.
H ow else can we explain the negativity?
R eminiscent of Rome
I n the time of antiquity.
S ad to say that hate does still roam,
T earing apart the members of a family.
I mmerse yourself in prayer to atone
A nd build a holy community,
N ever looking back at that dry bone.

A Conversation with God

Me to God:
I'm sleeping but awake
I'm weeping but I am filled with joy
I don't know but I am aware
I pray but still fall prey to that evil snare
I am not worthy but God loves me
I feel troubled but the Spirit sustains me
I do my best but God puts this to the test
I shirk my Cross but I know that's not best
I should pray more but the devil distracts
I see clearly but the world attracts
I try to listen to God but I know already
I try to lie to myself but it is so unsteady
I command my world but it's awfully cold
I'm squirming but God says I'm bold
I try and try but my heart cries to Heaven
I doubt and complain but I hear the lesson
I get angry but I am trying to love
I get nasty but I want to be a gentle dove
God responds:
Remove the "but" replace it with "and"
this is the battle of this worldly endeavor
This keeps you humble,
this struggle will not be forever

A Conversation with My Soul

> Can one ask questions
> of their soul?
> Yes, if one be so bold,
> what shall your question be of me?
> Is there but one love
> so true it hurts,
> and causes one to pains
> unbearable?

Unbearable you say? What is meant by your declaration? That you would prefer to love less, a love that you can bear without the heart and soul?

Yes! One that is but an ease to walk with, like a stroll with an autumn breeze while the sun kisses my cheek on the eve of a love spring.

Ah, but you ask for a lot less than true love. You beg to settle with a lie told a million times for true love cannot be contained as such. To do so, will drive you to insanity and vanity will be your new romance.

Why speak so candidly and honestly to me? Do you not see that I am afraid of the surrender that true love requires of me?

Ah, that sweet surrender is required a thousand times, for it is only thus that you shall find a kindred spirit worthy of thee to love thee as it must.

Tis I that asked a fair question and deny me you did not, so I must be thankful for your honesty. If you would be so kind to indulge me another?

Why it is your soul you ask, and you can ask a hundred thousand times, and I cannot deny thy request. Be bold or gentle in your request, according to what you can handle from me for what will come forth is honesty.

If I choose to love a little or extravagantly, what will become of me?

You ask of me to swing broadly in my answer to thee, is there fear that you already know what you ask of me but wanting for an acceptable compromise for thyself? Posing this question as if to soften your emotional demise, or to grant you permission to accept the rise of your awakened passion of your true hidden love?

Do tell, you must answer for are you not mine? Are you not me and I, you? I command an answer of you. What will become of my life if I surrender my love to true love and what ills await me if I deny my love?

One begets the other, depending on your choices. I am here with you always, just as true love with all its beauty and wonder but alas, most choose to love less. Never to have lived love to the fullest, thus cheating yourself of what is expected of us. This is to experience and share in true love without regard to the self. This is life's wealth.

> To deny this rich and fruitful love with something less,
> is to stab your heart and soul a thousand times.
> Slowly killing your spirit,
> replacing it with a vanity
> that lives only to love itself,
> making you disappear in it.

All Clear

I scream into the wind
a message of revival,
but the wind blows it back into my mind.
I need to focus on my own survival.

Staring into my heart
I see a very fragile existence,
coincidental in part.
It is unrecognizable persistence.
I have a tendency to contradiction
and I find comfort in futile piety
as I attempt to capture addiction,
running away from insanity.

As I run in place in circles,
I reach into my soul for the answers
only to find the darkness encircles,
as my screams find evil enhancers.

An inner struggle, battling day and night.
I wander with my spirit
but eventually turning to fright,
while warring to endure it.

What will I become in this life,
if my battle is lost before the war starts?

I'm chased by strife,
while my morality farts.
The stench of defeat is in the air.
I cry and shed a tear
and then I'm made aware,
Jesus gives the all clear!

Yesterday, today, and tomorrow
I remember the promise,
God's love is in escrow.
I should not be a doubting Thomas!

America Are You Free?

America the beautiful,
not through the eyes of the delusional.
You hem and haw
awaiting your master to caw,
no matter the truth
you accept the coup.

America, the home of the brave?
Not in this day, as you crave
the lies of a master deceiver.
The ultimate unbeliever!

America, the home of the free?
How long lasting is this spree?
Depends how many plays make believe.
Depends on how many misbelieve.

Truth takes courage.
The truth does encourage,
the extraordinary feat.

Lies discourage.
Lies do encourage,
the extraordinary deceit.

An Evil Pep Rally

What shall I plunder today?
The love belonging to another?
Shall I steal the will of my brother?
I know, I want to take your hope away!
I am who they used to call God's Light.
An endless fight within a fight.
Try with all your might,
but I win all your fright.
I beckon you with a delightful whisper,
and entice you with intimate pleasures.
Beginning with an ignorant insight
of love's real and truthful delights.
With you bored and confused,
Angry, and aloof,
you provide for me a fertile soil
for my elaborate, personalized turmoil.
I command your attention
with division and destruction.
Your endless fornication with pride
opens for me the opportunity
to hang you from the gallows
with sin as your noose,
and gossip as your ruse.
You, distracted from true love,
offer me a way into your thoughts.

Listen to what I say,
listen to what should be your way,
listen to the all-important you,
listen, listen for evil's impromptu lessons
designed just for you.
They divest you from your righteous crown.
You are becoming my personal clown
in this circus show of ill contempt!
How I love your weak mind,
and lack of empathy.
How I love your hunger for vainglory
and appetite for everything unholy.
What fertile soil to plant turmoil.
What fertile ground for a profound foil,
of a loving heart!
While I sell you the make believe,
that you are so very smart.
A timeless charmer,
I peddle sin to the lowest bidder.
While I watch God's perfection wither,
one at a time.
You become all mine.
LOL and LMAO.
Welcome to hell Yo!

Another Day

My fairy godmother whispers charms
in a brilliant runaway song.
I sway to the music of a runaway beat,
and I slow dance with my shadow.
Time stands still to race away,
and my destiny hides in a cave.

I wander in wonder,
and ponder an afterthought
wrought with guilty obsession.
Entangled in my own web of lies,
I compromise with doubt and wisdom.

Arriving to say goodbye is hello,
and I told you so returns the gotcha.
How can we care when we do not?
How can we love when we cannot?
When does a lie become true?
When do people decide to be undecided
but agree to decide about blue.

We careen into the out of control,
and race back towards the beginning.
Bells toll, but it is not for church.

The cock crows,
and I turn over.
The cock crows,
and I stumble into denial.
The cock crows,
and I retreat into a bitter awareness.

Here I have two choices:
Play and horseplay?
but none of these pretend to know me,
just try to define me.

Carried away is my new normal,
and normal left the building yesterday.
Eyes closed and reopened,
another day.

Be the Light

Dancing and flickering in the night,
fright envelopes the light
but the dark cannot consume
for the light cannot assume
it knows the way out.

Enveloped in light
I cannot see past the darkness.
I keep moving forward
as the night breaks with each step I take.
The light reveals what is exposed
but the darkness keeps everything a secret
until the light sets the secret free.

This light will one day shine upon everyone,
exposing every dark shadow,
and revealing what was done
in the secret of the night.

Blinded by the light
darkness cannot cause anymore fright.
The light leads your way out of the night,
and you can choose to be this light for others.

Be What I Am Meant to Be

There comes a time
Maybe another in a lifetime
Which seems like it takes my breath away
I gasp for air underwater
And realize that was the wrong reaction
I should have held on just a little longer
When it was safe to breathe
I start to choke on what I did not need
Greed of something I desire
I start to panic
How do I get out of this mess I created
This mess that found its way inside of me
Anxiety and fear take hold
And I take another breath
As I go deeper
It gets colder
Fear and panic alert my mind
The end of my time is near
What will I do
Float to the dark blue peace at the bottom
Or fight to the light I can still see
I tell myself
Don't you see
This is how things play out daily with me
Struggle and choice
Choice and struggle
I can try to live in a bubble
But will that bubble always float

Especially when there are others
Trying to run me over with their boat
Boats filled with privilege and advantage
Like the surfer that cuts through waves
I can navigate my life
I just have to stop fixating on the grave
And live like the free and the brave
Courage in me that I know who I am
And what I am meant to be

Celebrate Life

Once life resided within,
with all of life's rambling.
Happy, sad, accomplishing,
failing or compromising.
Much more, of course,
for it is a life force.
We speak, we act, we frown and smile.
Why most can even walk a mile,
but ask it to love and only some say yes.
They say I love while playing it like chess,
making strategic moves
and predicting countermoves.
Yes, there is dead life
creating so much strife
and missing out on loving life.
Some get hooked on phonics,
others on the digital platonic.
Making the error between the physical,
and the mystical aspects of sex.
Some get roped into addiction,
which can become a lifelong affliction.
Few, though many, get it.
It is the few, not the many, that own it.
I speak of the wonder of loving love,
for the abundant life you find in it.

Confusion

In this, the end of time, we find the profusion
of confusion and illusion.
All be told, it is the fusion
of collusion and pollution.

The strategy to confuse our absolution
is the allusion of confusion.
Taking advantage of our love malnutrition.

The only ammunition?
A great sense of intuition
in Divine intervention!
Pay close attention,
or suffer the pain of broken resolution.

Limit your adoration of every emotion
that motions you to a notion
of senseless commotion.
That draws you into a devotion of lore
regarding the promotion
of spreading
temptation and illusion.

Corona la Llorona

Estos tiempos no se ignora,
porque a la gente no le importa.

No se quedan en casa
porque solo le molesta.

Que lastima.

Mientras el hospital se llena
y la gente queja
porque no lo acepta.

Ya no salgan para fuera
si no,
se espera recibir,
la Corona.

Ya, después te dicen a ti, la llorona.

¿Cuál Será Tú Gritó?

Uno grita
"El dolor es mucho, ¿cómo lo aguanto?"
La vida es muy dolorosa
para seguir en esta manera.

                        Sin conocer que es la vida que eligió,
                        pero no quiere cambiar sus hábitos
                        por pensar que son pocitos
                        los pecados comparados con otros.

El error erótico del diablo
que muchos le han dado un pase.
Fácil entrar en esta manipulación
si uno acepta la contradicción
que una mentira conocida
se acepta cómo verdad.

                        La vida dice mucho,
                        si eres grande o chico
                        uno sabe más con más edad
                        y la tempestad de la dolorosa vida
                        lo sigue igual.

Para cambiarlo para lo bueno
el grito debe ser
"¡Diosito ayúdame, no puedo solo!"

                        El Rey del Cielo te oirá
                        y pronto llegará el refresco
                        único a Dios, Hijo y Espíritu Santo.

Daffodil

A whirlwind of time stands still
    but my mind never will
        be still
I reach for a poisoned pill
    and wait for the thrill
        of emotional distill.
I'm whisked away from my will
    and my heart surrenders a shrill
        it is found dishabille
Like running backward uphill
    doesn't take any special skill
        only a weak will
            makes a mountain out of a molehill
                and rejects love like falling downhill
                  while welcoming the kill
Embracing love in this standstill
    becomes my only hope to fulfill
        my desire to bloom like the daffodil
First to bloom from winter's chill
    and a new beginning
        a refill in this life's steel mill.

Depression Has Lied to You

If I leave this earth today, what will people say? It grieves me to no end that so much of our lives is pretend. We put on a good show about what everyone should know, and we succumb to that melancholy humdrum. Dancing like that monkey on a string to the rhythm of the monotonous drum and to societies every liking. We escape into our solitude, the one the mind can't ignore but with the usual platitude; boring and unsure. We yell "Help!" but no one listens because we only yell it on the inside and hidden from view. Persistence is the nature of our existence, but we don't dive into the darkness of our mind or examine the shadows of our heart. We start in some ways, eager to meet who we really are but we only go so far. We turn around at the sign of trouble pretending to not see that real me standing on the corner trading a lie for a trick, or a trick for a lie. I'm trying to buy into the sublime line of only the lonely can survive in real time, because the world has gone crazy. There are supernatural creatures behind those chained doors that you put away so long ago in order to restore a torn soul. Why did you tamper with the chain that keeps you from the insane? Why did you want to meet them again? It has only been too long to venture past that assurance of people saying "It's going to be alright" only to find everyone's druthers are the same. Every season is like the other, bored with reason and our most famous line "I am not the caretaker for my brother." The examination of self is like anything else, one by one and alone to moan and groan. No one else can examine what's in us, they only know what we show them, the pun within us. Pretend not to worry and showing only the glory of a transient space where I park my immoral grace. Ignoring my virtue in some hideaway torture subspace. I will break any trace of that immaculate foreign race of plunder and shame I call on to proclaim a grace not my own. I'm all alone. Naked and ashamed of this circular insane waning only when I want to proclaim and name that wanted shame. To wear it like a trophy, this only the lonely atrophy of wanting only to think of me, myself and I. I wear that lie! I dream to die a relief, a sigh. This endless struggle to the want of death but not wanting to take that last breath, just circling round and round. Who can I call to help me with this mess, no one really knows the moves to this supernatural game of three-dimensional chess! Ah, but there is one. One who knows all the moves and grooves to the only truth. A truth of what really lies behind those dark thoughts in your mind. We are not alone as the monsters tell you in song, we were never meant to be all alone; we choose this on our own. We are called to be clever and endeavor into the multitude of love, to become as gentle as the dove.

The answer you will find when you dive deep inside seems so simple, it is nothing but everything having to do with love! Not the kind you steal with a deal of this or that but something real and does not engage in any form of tit for tat. This real love comes from only one place, and it's not the property of humanity. It was a gift, a triumphant present of love and sacrifice to suffice the price for our love of death's enticement. Claim this gift by repairing the drift you committed and return triumphantly to the one, the only, in all his divine glory, my Father, who art in heaven, hollowed be Your name!

Down the Rabbit Hole

Hey! Hey! Over here.
Let me whisper sweet nothings in your ear.
You can trust me my dear.
I want only the best for you, do you hear?
Listen to my voice and don't you fear
      I will be finished soon, making it clear
      that you don't have to adhere
      to the truth, just pay that puppeteer.
The slick serenity of being steered,
      causing you to attend his premier
      of haughty laughter and tantalizing jeer.
It only costs you a soul to sinfully endear
      and make it disappear.
I must be sincere,
      you are easily led with a sinister sneer.
Be careful not to leave it here,
      turn away from the death-daddy's career
      and follow the Truth and be sincere
      because, if not, it's a mighty deep scary rabbit hole my dear.

God, What Would You Have Me Do?

Be faithful to your true nature, living in communion with God.
Learn to be Spiritually mature with faith the seed, and love the sod!
It will spring forth hope for sure and beckon the roughshod.
Beckon them so as to procure, the transformation of those misled by fraud.
Make those sacrifices that makes you pure, honoring that Holy Squad.
        The Father, the Son and the Holy Ghost!
He will continue to lead and teach,
Do not be afraid, nor procrastinate.
For if you do as He says and you beseech,
God will bless you and make you, His oblate.
Just as His disciples were told to go teach,
To a world full of hate.
So too, we are called for outreach
For the lost and those who obfuscate.
Let love be your only speech,
And be complete in your holy state!

Good Luck Today

Those that say if you pray
> It will lead you astray,
> well, what do you think is happening today?

Could it be because you think this way?
> Hey! No way!
> You can't have it this way and that way.

You must choose a way
> Led astray or pray?
> And expect the foray, either way.

Difference being peace or dismay!
> Good luck today.
> Nay, I say
> God be with you this day.

Happy Fourth of July

Some say this country is about to die,
especially when we glorify the lie.

Deception is our new affection.

Inviting intolerance to the dance,
courting violence in this lustful romance.

Right is wrong and wrong is right,
this is our new indulgent delight.

Love is buried in our heart's sanctuary,
releasing its power is quite contrary.

The devil convinced us it is unnecessary.

We have been led astray from the way,
the way of love in love for love.

We don't have to be a broken token
of the evil game of shame, and insane.

We can mend our way through this day
by allowing love a glowing end play.

Allowing love the leading part in your heart.

I Pray to be Refined

I awake from the darkness of my mind
    Wondering how I lost all this time
    And how I got left behind
I did not realize I committed a crime
What crime you ask can make me blind
The kind of a corrupt social paradigm
One with a history of misleading mankind
Can I awaken my heart from this pastime
Or am I convicted to be unkind
Depends on your choices every time
    You make a decision with an evil bind
The way to escape is to be disinclined
    To continue your evil begrime
Look to Heaven and pray you be refined!

i want to escape

heartbroken but alive,

with nothing to say

swimming in circles

wishing i would be drawn in

of my certain destruction

once happy and full of joy

loving me walked away

i want to escape my stranger

i choose to ignore

when it is behind closed doors

i remember love awakened

a spark touched by joy

the damage of love lost before

i walk alone

a hollow shell

i want to escape my stranger

around whirlpools

feeling the excitement

i want to escape my stranger

all stripped away

with nothing else to say

a melody so sweet

love is too painful

i want to escape my stranger.

ignited by the unknown

but unable to restore

Jesus Got You

I can't help what you do,
I can only control what I do.
Isn't it true that whatever I do
will also affect you?
Isn't it also true, that whatever you do
will influence me too?
What to do?
I do desire to consider this through.
It is between me and you!
There is a connection between the two,
and it is that they are called to be true.
It makes me think of you,
and it makes you think of me too!
How true!
Destined to always think anew.
A fresh start between me and you,
and a love-to-love others too!
What a great idea!
ACHOO
What is wrong with you?
You got the flu?
Go away, I may catch it too!
Don't freak out, because He got you.
Who?
Jesus, that's who!
In this life and the afterlife too.

My Kryptonite

dark and warm
enveloped in a cold shell
wanting to ride the wind
everything stands still
and i try to catch my spirit
it is on the loose outside of me
only coming home to rest
when it has run out of everything else
it searched the world for another home
because my heart had grown too familiar
used and abused by an illusion
and a fusion of hate and disgust
it found trust in pride and lust
foraging in the dampness of nowhere places
racing to an erotic complacency
it found me another vice
and dragged it back home
to meet the other lies
those demons i have hidden and living inside
Now i have a riot going on led by pride
while greed, lust and envy
ride the ride to never ever places
inside my mind.
what time is it
what day is it
i have lost track of time
as these spirits drown out
the song of truth

make believe becomes my reality
as my spirit leads me to insanity
i gasp and claw for love
except that i cannot hold on
as i fall upside-down
my world starts to move sideways
never again to look for help
just stuck and moving my life
from side to side
as i prepare for another fall
when my spirit goes on another turbulent ride
in a futile search for its missing piece
looking for a release
that will never please its master
my spirit screams at my soul
and we become two
living on the same bone
in a broken home of fear and despair
and decorated with fake teardrops
home sweet horrible home
i am all alone and crowded
my strangers i know all too well
feeling weak i try to fight
but my wandering spirit
is my kryptonite

Panic in a Pandemic

A manic monkey riding on a donkey
Can this be our reality in perpetuity
Our society lacking social ingenuity
A clown juggling a lie around town
People screaming out their dreaming
Leaning into dismay while they run away
With problems inventing their emblems
Only to cry to the why
Extremely distraught by the rot
Rot of the exceptionalism of capitalism
While the might of fright
Incorporates the ingrates
Leading in the fight of greed
While everyone else dispels the infidels
Touting the grand beginnings of winnings
Not knowing the trophy is atrophy
And the glorious reward, precarious
If only hearts would soften in parts
This could be a stalwart start
To help us all endeavor to good behavior
I can hope upon the love of true love
For it is true and will not misconstrue
Some lie or gesture into
die you pester
What will become of us if we fuss
Over how much I can love you and such
Instead of how I can kill your will
What a thought but today a naught

People do not want to hear the good cheer
They only want to be lonely
To be scared and angry about things impaired
Instead of working on the solutioning
We pastime on the waste time
And debate the hate
Embracing all the morality erasing
And finding comfort in the binding
All tied up and frustrated while we waited
In the darkness of absoluteness
The monster and sponsor dance in a the satan dance

Perplexed

Perplexed and vexed at what may come
        is only wasted energy to harbor a home
                in your heart
Let love reign
    this is where you should start
        not with lies fed to your mind
           which makes you blind
                to the trickery of treachery

Self-Absorbed

I'm in control of my suffering and pain.
I gain the cosmos for the immensity of the intensity of my sorrow. The moon cries with me while the seas rise to the occasion. The darkness envelopes me like the air filling every pore only to score more shadows cast by the minor light of the night sky. Night lasts forever, time never seeming to drive by to pick me up and whisk me away to the drive-in of my life. Relieved for the no-show because you never know if the reel will be a silent black and white or an all-color peep show with loud thunder foiled by doubt. Wishing that it could be a musical of grandeur and a peek of the hereafter. Only to be disappointed by screams of fear and feelings of disaster. I mean can I just have one dream of eating my favorite ice cream?! Maybe I can dream that I can fly, and I can forget how to cry about the ordinary. I whisper to my tears about my fears to maneuver through the maze ablaze with lost dreams and empty hopes. Where can I drop off this irony of simplicity and replace it with the complexity and courage of love? When can I open my eyes from my worldly slumber and stare into the eyes of the true mystery of the divine where my heart should roam with all of mankind? Soon my dear, very soon you can swoon into a room built just for you with just enough room for flowers that mask the decay but play a part in your play on pity. What comes next is anyone's guess, depends on that game of chess you played and the moves you chose to make in the wake of an attack. A frontal assault or flanked, what did you do? Escape, counterattack or withdraw, and declared a draw? What happens next is anyone's guess. Did you dress for success in virtue or declare your demise in some evil vice, like drinking from a flask of lies? The walls of the tollbooth where you slumber start to move in and the air is no more. What comes next, one can only wonder, especially as I ponder my lifetime of plunder, which stole my heart. When I arise will it be to my eternal demise or to the glory of a promise for not wasting my life? Make that U-turn from torn and broken and make your way to the road that does not lead you astray, but takes you on a journey of joy and the absence of dismay. Fight not for your life, but that of another not as fortunate as you. You have the time to sing your blues, what about that misfortune of the one who has run out of tears and cannot afford the tears for you?

Senseless Squabbling

The sparrow said to the duck,
    I don't like the way you quack,
        as he swooped close to his head.
You make silly noises, said the duck.
    You sound like a cricket that got stuck
        and then starts screeching.
The wise owl, intrigued with the quarrel,
    lifted his talon and shook the squirrel.
        He shook it until the squirrel barked.
The sparrow and the duck shut up,
    and stared at each other while thinking,
        that is really messed up!
The simple gesture of a wise owl,
    reveals that their squabble has run afoul.

Sin

Evil of a different tier
brings to my eye a tear
only to fear
what lies dormant here.

It tugs a string
and it begins the fling.
Offering fruits of suffering,
deceiving to believe it's nothing.

Beware the snare
it doesn't compare
to your share
of loathing and despair.

It is a dangerous dance,
but at first glance
you see a radiance
of power and elegance.

Only to be fooled,
and ridiculed!

Snooze You Lose

I'm a sinner, you're a sinner.
There is no beginner to a winner.
Hard work and practice are what it takes
to diminish all those mistakes.
Running full speed into a wall,
that's what lies do, and make you fall.
Falling up the stairs,
that's what pride does, and no one cares.
Tripping over your misstep,
spite does this, causing one to overstep.
Slapping yourself silly,
foolishness does this, going willy-nilly.
Laughing and crying,
sin does this because you're not trying.
Praying and fasting,
righteousness does this, it is everlasting!
Pick and choose,
faith does this, you snooze you lose.

Survivor

Everything is different today
Especially from what it was yesterday
Explaining the difference is meaningless
Experience is one's own reality
Eluding your demons is a daily task
Empathy should be your lure
Encouragement a choreographed chore
Expectation should not be nurtured
Endeavor to realize your good nature
Eradicate habits leading to your spirit indentured
Extol the love and faithfulness of God
Employ mastery and reject the odd
Enthusiastically speak of Love
Evoke and invoke the Holy Spirit
Engrossed are all who draw near It
Efforts to be good and holy
Emulate our intended glory
Enthroned within our Savior
Exposes our failure
Enjoyment is your own private fruit
Enlightenment a shared pursuit
Examining your secret ward
Endowment is your reward
Engraving grace upon your soul
Exclaiming the greatness of our God be told

The Great Fall

God smiled on His Creation
for He saw in it His perfection.
Blessing the seventh day and making it holy.
But then saw that man was lonely.
He took man's rib from his body
to create for him an antibody
for his lonely heart.
A pair that would never part.
Things were divine
as they enjoyed the fruit of the vine.
Only one fruit will surely smite,
But the fallen Angel once God's brilliant light,
he called to Eve and whispered,
it's just a small bite.
I promise you will not be injured.
A bite she did take,
and invited her spouse to partake.
Pride led to disobedience,
death entered on their expedience.
What shame!
Playing the blame game.
Needless to say,
today is no different
because that serpent is still at play
and mankind has a problem with being reverent.
Jesus, nailed to a cross
was the payment for this obnoxious
double-cross full of loss.

My message is this,
the only redress
is to win this holy game of chess!
Turn to the only one who can save you from your duress.
Satan got you into this mess,
high time you ask for forgiveness.
It is God who can offer you wholeness.
His heavenly holiness
can offer you rest.
So, ignore that pest
when he puts you to the test.
Tempting and inviting
which only leads to dividing.
His game was clear from the start,
he wants to rob your heart.
So be stalwart
or to the liar's joy,
you will fall apart.
Stop being his throwaway toy!

The Light

A ray of light is born of its source,
radiant and illuminating is its force,
darkness comes to change the course
diminishing it and making life worse.
Too often this leads to a divorce,
or a self-destructive intercourse
which love cannot endorse.
The light, diminished, feels remorse
and seeks the chandelier concourse.
A chandelier illuminating and shinning radiantly enforce.
Light to shine like a winning racehorse,
assisting and lifting the light to reinforce.
The light, in love, reunites with its Source,
thus, bestowing a vital force
for the love and charity workforce.

Transcendence

I search for relevance
While I experience
A society's heart addicted to decadence
I ponder the elegance
Of love and forgiveness
In a world that demands evidence
Beyond a preponderance
That life is no happenstance
While we all live by chance
In the fog of a prideful arrogance
Brought upon us by the naive brilliance
Of a people eager to serve reluctance
With such eloquence
And with an ill-conceived persistence
Eager to the dominance
Of forces that demand crassness
Because it enslaves righteousness
And lays waste all truthfulness
To the acceptance
Of hopelessness
But then there is a light of excellence
That shines in brightness
Which beckons one with openness
And invites us to fruitfulness
With a peaceful awareness
That captivates our playfulness
And eradicates any boastfulness

But rather excites the humbleness
Of our soul and a mindfulness
That we do not exist in aloneness
But we coexist in oneness
And are invited to an eternal blissfulness
And is this not life's existence
To reach a fullness
And completeness
A transcendence
Otherwise, life is just a fretful trance

Tomorrow Today Yesterday

       Run behind chase,
                      and improvise.
       Command your actions
             to command your thoughts.
       Paralyze your heart,
             until you need a jump start.
       Dragging your feet apart,
             you hoist yourself to the bottom.
       Upside down vs not quite anywhere,
             you dilly-dally with intention.
       Integrity has lost the reason,
             you turn to bellicose treason.
       Remarks on silence go dead,
             and what was once said is ignored.
       Aggression is the new I love you,
             and empathy is taken prisoner.
       It is raining sideways,
             and the wind has been captured.
       The mountains shiver in fright,
             and might withers away.
       Cowardice becomes elegance.
             hypocrisy, the common language.
       Fear draws you near,
             and whispers, I have a big stick.
       You lose control,
             and capture chaos.

Very few cling to love and hope,
                        and marvel in its majesty.
Tomorrow becomes today,
                        and yesterday seems far away.

We wait

Oh, how my heart longs for Him.
It was only day before last he washed my feet.
Yesterday they drove spikes through His every limb.
I did not expect this would end in defeat!
Why are things so grim?
A week ago, we were part of the elite,
entering Jerusalem while the crowd chanted a praising hymn.
Now we sit in fear, closed up in retreat.
Was this all on a whim?!
Can I trust in the God to Jesus to us entreat?
If He was the Son, where were His Cherubim?
This whole matter, so indiscreet!
I want to worship Him,
I want to shout in the street!
But what will I say when things look so dim?
That God's plan is so offbeat?
A resurrection seems awfully slim.
He taught He was the tree and we His branches, destined to accrete.
But today, I feel, how did He win?
I will wait and be discreet,
what will happen tomorrow when,
He promised no defeat,
He promised us a win.
So, for today I will retreat,
into Him,
for my faith tells me this story is incomplete!

What a Choice!

Untie that knot that breaks your heart.
Look up to Heaven for a new start.
The sadness and madness
that fights for your attention
takes on the breath of frustration
which explains all the evil demonstration.

Apart from the love that exists in some simple beings, there is no taste for the haste of moral teachings. Bored in a life of misery but too complacent to bond with our history that bore in civility a particular mystery. Peel back time to find that crime that led us here and you will understand we are in the prime of our own sensationalism. In our reach and quite at ease is a pleasant atonement but instead we desire to please ourselves uniquely with our evil betrothment to falsities and crude ire.

Some dine on this fine swine.

Believing in their dark hearts it's all mine, and there is absolutely no crime. No reason to whine. It is only you, the one who has nothing, that wants my king, but he is mine and mine alone because you cannot afford him with your sublime rhyme of childish gibberish trying to foretell this point in time. Those sweet lullabies of heavenly splendor will not purchase for you the indecency of your tendencies because it is impossible for love to live your perceived emergencies of need and want of what is fraught with anger, lust, hate and despair.

Oh, such the pair! Good and evil!

One seemingly lustrous and the other amply ambitious while we naïvely see both as ambiguous. Which one you choose to see in what light, and with all your might is a telltale of what is in your heart, your very soul, who scolds you with the other if you let it be so. While one is steady the other is ready to pounce as you bounce from one to the other as if you have all the time to recover. Why bother? You must ponder alone or with your brother only to discover there is but one truth, the one everyone seeks, and that truth is love and there is no other!

Your Right to Fight a Spiritual Rape

At times, when demons win their escape,
you experience a spiritual rape.
A tumble into that gaping black hole
that lies in the middle of your soul.
Suddenly, and violently
the real you is vehemently ignored
while you become a toy of deceit.
You act out in a vacuum of illicit glamour,
knowing and not knowing,
that you don't have to choose defeat
or sound a retreat.
Much like those comfy clothes
the violence becomes innocence,
because your stripped of reasoning
when the beckoning arrives
and deprives you of recognizing lies.
You submit without a choice,
your unable to find a spiritual voice.
While we have the power to resist
it is presented as this irrational bliss
that seems impossible to resist.
How can I dismiss anything such as this?
How can I be and be me,
as God created me to be?
This is no simple task to win eternity!

Alas,
it is because of this,
Jesus departed His throne
and arrived in the way we all arrive,
in order to claim us for God alone.
He shed all His royalty
to come helplessly and in poverty,
as a stranger to His home
and born to roam.
When we think we have no choice,
when we think we've lost our voice,
remember His promise to the wise
because there is no compromise.
He won the worthy soul
that uses their choices
to reclaim their role
as children of light,
cutting through all the lying noises
and choosing His might to fight
those lying voices in your head.
Ignite your light,
welcome the Paraclete as your promised right,
to the children of Light.

Salt

Have you ever tasted bland salt? Since salt holds its properties for so long, it is rare to find someone who finds that the salt in the cupboard has gone bad. Salt is a preservative; it kills microbes and draws water out. So why did Jesus refer to salt while instructing us to be the salt of the earth? Well, I am no theologian and there are many others that can elaborate and provide you with more answers than me. What I can do is tell you why I chose this title for a group of my poems.

We know that salt is a preservative, it adds flavor to foods, it heals, it makes you thirsty, it helps our bodies retain fluids to keep us from dehydrating and oddly enough it dehydrates to preserve foods. Anyway, the attributes I want to focus on have to do with preservative, flavor and purification.

We all have gifts that are given to us by our Creator. As disciples of Christ, we are told that we are the salt of the world. In my spiritual journey I often pray and contemplate this mandate given to us by our Lord and Savior. I want to listen, to hear, to examen, to discern and to act. I noticed that some of the poems that were inspired in me were rather salty. I mean, they have a stinging truth to them and since I am not exempted from the messages in these poems, they stung. Some stung a little and others were like pouring salt into an open wound. I choose to look at these poems as preservatives where the message is about pointing out the moral decay of society or in the individual because we have become sin infected. It is spreading and people are turning to their own truth, whatever best suits our ego, vanity, and pride. A lust for power and control has taken hold.

There are other poems that give a full and delightful flavor to the message. Some say that as Christians we are to live so purely as to be a blessing to others, enriching their encounter by experiencing Jesus' love through our love, charity and service. There are still other poems that the message has a more healing trait and helps identify the sickness while attempting to convince us of the best, and often, the only treatment: *Truth, Love & Light*.

I often wonder that maybe Jesus said that we are the salt of the earth to remind us how valuable we are to God and to the world considering the *Truth, Love, & Light* that He was instilling in us. There was a time where salt was so expensive only the rich could buy it. Now, the world has cheapened it, much like our sinful desires have cheapened us by contaminating our salt, making us bland and tasteless. Truth and love lead us to light, and when our spirit matures we can be that full flavor, one that preserves the truth, and witness to our purification in such a way that our lives become fruitful and full of love.

If salt is what you're meant to be to this earth, time to consider a rebirth!

20/20 Fake and Phony

in the blink of an eye
you lie
the wise sigh
and are moved to cry for you
while you deny
and throw a tizzy
that something must be awry
unable to control your pride
a snide leader you cannot abide
the fact that we choose to chide
and want to end this carnival ride
now some say you will run again
Teddy tried in vain
he never got over his chagrin and pain
of trying to win over the hearts and minds again
best to take your leave
something hard for you to conceive
that we wanted a reprieve
from your love to deceive
heads are spinning
that the other guy is winning
this only sends your folks careening
into misgiving
because you lie and claim
I'm winning
I'm winning

so sad to have the fake king panicking
while stirring up your fanatic following
into a wild rage of enrage
and a wallowing hallowing
of our democratic golden age
by commanding them to disengage from sanity and reality
oh what a shame
this is the age of the insane game
now will you realize this was mundane
no second coming of the divine
whoever started that had too much wine
time to change the channel on this reality show of the art of the undermine
While my fellow Christians struggle
to juggle the hypocrisy jungle
that God has somehow lost control
what malicious vitriol has captured your soul
please turn to prayer and not to that demerol
We have enough zombie addicts
and we need all of you if we are to follow Jesus' edicts to love one another
and heal us from satan's evil antics
let hope and love enter your heart
let us start to be stalwart for love
be so much in love with love
that your love and light shines bright
and your love becomes synonymous
with hope for those you encounter
and they are drawn into the hope of love for love's sake
we rebuke all the delusion caused by the fake and phony

A House Divided

A nation in shame,
with all to blame for this game.
It's all about faming the shame blame!
The Office has defaulted to a man you can't tame.
Not taking the responsibility with dignity
while lies are told about lies told on the twitty.
If I say it enough it will be so, silly!
From the office of the free comes a glee
for foe and disdain for my bro, where does this all go?
While others, what is their focus?
To judgement and a curse too boot.
What a hoot!
All blind to the rotten root
of the irrelevant.
What has become of us?
What is the propellant?
Too extravagant
that we invent the drug dependent of want.
A zombie we create.
Is this our fate with hate?
Oh, but watch the epidemic grow out of control.
I'm sure you are asking yourself but what of myself?
Cold!
Don't be the twelfth!
Judas kissed Christ once for the betrayal
Not we all,
we do it again and again to prevail.
Same as the pain, our evil avail!

Pain, blood, sweat, and a crawl
while all we do I$ brawl?!
Be of peace, just cease
with the word abuse
and squall of lies
this will be your demise
but heaven awaits those who love.
Sing about true love
forever told
as the treasure trove
of the cries
of the wise.

A Joker

A joker who plays poker
    Always the croaker,
        Grumbling, foreboding evil stoker!
        All the while the bully
        All the while sully
            With evil as the pulley.
                We play the game or look away in shame,
                What is the harm to my name?
                Everything when you cause
              or support the pain.

Am I My Brother's Keeper?

Woe is me goes the plea,
and with such a great energy!
All I hear is gnashing of teeth
and a great bewail
I don't hear a simple thing like
How are you, my dear?
My neighbor far and near,
how can I be of service to you?
How can I bring you good cheer?
Cover my face and keep my space?
What the heck is wrong with you?!
Don't you have any clue?!
The state is trying to muzzle you!
I ain't a dope on a rope,
nope, nope!
I got guns that say I gotta say,
I do not have to stay and play.
This is all a conspiracy
but what you don't see
my lost brother and sister
is that the only idiots are you and me.
You for just being a self-absorbed
know it all,
me for listening to you
berate and gyrate
and spreading your hate.
What a shame that this is no game
it's all about humans being disposable.
How can this not be deplorable?

We knew this day was coming.
We play games where we kill, kill, kill
We watch TV and it is kill, kill, kill
We do drugs and kill, kill, kill
We get drunk and kill, kill, kill
We get mad crazy and kill, kill, kill
We get emotional and kill, kill, kill
We go to a school and kill, kill, kill
We have sex in lust and kill, kill, kill
We get greedy and kill, kill, kill
We get hangry and kill, kill, kill
And now,
We get bored and kill, kill, kill.
Oh, what sadness in these last days
but what all should remember is we all pay!
One way or that way
we don't get away
from the other side of that kill.
I mean, all you have to do is stand still
and kill, kill, kill.
We've made it that easy
because we forget how to love,
do you see?
How this all works out to be?
Kill, kill, kill has a great many type
It's not always the loss of life
It can take other forms
Like killing souls
Like killing hope
Like killing goals
Like killing laughter
Like killing sanity
Like killing health
Like killing empathy
Like killing dreams

Like killing charity
Like killing joy
Like killing truth
Like strangling faith.
Beware of the snare
of the 10empter$ glare!
Love, so that you don't become the killer
in a sinister
plot to devour
where the liar becomes the minister
just to attain the power
to tower
over mankind!

America is in Trouble

Greed is what this America heeds,
not morally good deeds.
It only allows a baron to succeed.
Might and power is declared
only achieved by humanity despaired.
What happened to the notion of communion
to build a more perfect union?
What is causing our implosion?
Many of you in your heart know,
it has all become some strange circus show.
Animals and clowns with no ringmaster,
only infighting to satisfy a lying master.
A liar from the beginning,
and winning,
like he did with that fruit,
so death could enter a perfect world.
The blind have always existed,
this is the only way the lie persisted.
If you are part of the blind,
how would you know you are in this bind?
You can't, you shan't
you will only plant, pant, and rant!
The only hope for this America
are the prayers from those who seek God's truth,
not the religiously uncouth.
Only proclaiming and claiming the name,
but forsaking Him for the insane.
But how would you know it?

It has eluded you because of the lie from a crafty liar
that has claimed you too.
You aren't special, except in your mind.
I know this sounds unkind but let's rewind,
you're the only reason you are where you are in your mind
and heart.
We are told that truth can be sought,
but not in that master that has always fought
and bought mankind with a lie.
Just so that we can die.
How can you know?!
You've been purchased with an ego.
And before you utter God bless you,
think of that commandment that says
I must love you no matter what!
But you have the most problem with that!
This is where you must start.
But how would you know?!
Most of you are enjoying the show!
So how can you possibly know?!
Your biggest sin is that you think this is the real show
and that it is primo.
The lie is in your ego.
The next problem is those who ignore,
or cannot be bothered in the score.
While you think you have no stake,
well this is your ultimate mistake!
"I do not care to partake
because it is all fake."
The battle is real my brother,
but only when your cage is rattled
do you stir into the battle.
But at this point you cannot empower,
because you were too lazy
or unconcerned to accumulate any real power.

So, you retreat and allow others to mistreat
while you remain discreet.
Your only hope is to call on the Paraclete.
We see from history,
pride comes before the fall,
at least those who live in love and spirit
will heed the call
to draw closer to God,
while fasting and praying
out of love and obedience
to mitigate this insidious
misdeed by the need
to mislead!
You are invited,
always have been.
Don't be so short-sighted
this is all about to careen
to something we have never seen.

Save yourself by not being so mean,
and no need to scream at each other.
Just learn to love your brother,
and Love one another!!

America's Tit for Tat

Hail to the unbelievable,
we wail the unachievable!
All the while, denouncing the achievable.
While solutions are conceivable,
we argue preposterously the inconceivable.
Gun down another,
and another,
and another.
Because, quite frankly, I care nothing about my neighbor.
While I pretend to be aghast,
we go nowhere fast.
We proclaim to worship and love God,
all the while we maintain the fraud.
We wail and scream,
a few hours pass, and we're back to the same scheme.
America the beautiful, we say.
Well, the curtain has been torn away!
We are in love with violence,
and only if it were in ignorance.
But this is not so,
we know the cost of this sinful show.
We leave the grieving to their own,
while we carry on with a fake moan.
America, home of the inventive brain?
Ha! It is just more of the insane.
America, home of the free?
Where we still hang a noose from a tree.
America, the beautiful?
Where we embrace the sinful.

Greed, power, and dominance,
this has become our intimate romance.
Kill the weak and ignore the poor,
don't like it? Let me show you the door.
Bickering, hate, and intolerance we cheer.
This has become music to our ear.
Corruption and lies,
is this what America now personifies?
Hypocrisy is the new standard of living,
and what is the new love but misgivings.
How much longer can we survive?
America is in an evil dive.
Religion suffers the same affliction,
enamored with its spiritual malnutrition.
Christianity is in the same calamity,
because we cannot love honestly.
Tit for tat,
this is where America is at.

Ammo for My Blunderbuss

Too cute by half,
    your greed and pride are dangerous.
Holding up the golden calf,
    your cause is still as monstrous.
While evil lets out a giggle and a laugh,
    proud of being so boisterous.
We no longer believe lying is a gaffe,
    we buy the lie as wondrous.
Hate, pride, and lies are my autograph
    so I take aim and fire like a blunderbuss.

Anticipating Love

In retrospect we lack respect.
We, the people, now expect respect
    without reciprocating.
We make demands of fanatic fans.
We issue commands that play our hand all the while, insinuating.
Yelling topsy-turvy, marred by my lying.
How can this be free for you and me?
All the while, speculating.
Any role doled out for love be told?
Any bold takers, or are we too cold
    and debilitating.
We gloat float opinions to take note.
We bloat our pride like the antidote
    all the while capitulating.
Love wins over sins and amends.
Twin sins, evil and hate
    slowly diminishing.
Love rebuilding, forgiving, fulfilling,
    anticipating.

Beyond Hopeless

Liar, liar your hair is on fire but your so used to it, you just don't care. Lips pursed and out comes your ire; lies upon lies with lies that ensnare and inspire without compare. Your clan happily and verily inspired to promote and shout your lying and ire. Using your power without compare promoting a one-man freak show for hire, designed on disrepair. Your ego and conceit knows no bounds neither do your worshipers while they act like clowns. There is not one with a frown for the lies upon lies worn like a crown, in this ultimate lying circus shown year-round. Claiming their virtue is a throne to own your own stone. Lying to hold on to power while your vanity claims the hour. America's heart is on display lying to save the day while people die and go astray. We want what we want without delay, with no sacrifice of lying today. This is what got us in this mess anyway! And likely will not change this power that enslaves this hour. People love their drama while reality shows are shaping our karma. We love it so we gave it our power. Where the liars and cheats once sour, are now sweet like honey, while they devour as they sit in their ivory tower. America is on fire with all these lies this is no surprise to the wise this madness was noticeably on the rise. People's intolerance with no compromise ignited the spark for the father of lies while we fanned the flames of our own demise. We are all to blame with our countless and seemingly harmless, white lies. We are going nowhere fast, ignoring our violent past. Turning to love is the only way out of this mess! People deserve the truth and a path for redress.

    Only then can we show that we are beyond hopeless.

Blind Sheep

Like sheep
                asleep
                                soul stripped naked
                  sacred
      exposed
                unopposed
                        to stand alone
       but together
                we roam
                      one groan
       after another
                                  no beginner
           in this affair,
                    a layer of lies
        a compromise
                    to not expose
                                the soul to a repose
         but to agitate
and aggravate
         the peace of mind
                slaying the kind
                           and worshipping
like suckling
        swine
                one at a time
                          to that eternal flame

oh, what a shame
                              the lying game,
            tag your it,
                    unfit
                              but claiming to wit
        lying to your heart
                    not really that smart
    considering the stakes
                        for your mistakes
            but too fascinated
                                        with the intimidated
                mastermind
        of the unkind,

                rewind
            don't be blind
            choose love
            seek God above
            receive true love
            stop following
            a stranger's voice
            hear Truth glowing
        but it must be a choice
            to rejoice
                in love

Checkmate

Is hate a human trait?
Is your smile just evil bait?
Do you entice others to berate?
Do you encourage the hate?
What about God's mandate?
What about Jesus telling us not to hate?
Why is it so hard for you to tolerate?
Why is your deviance so innate?
Why do you live to isolate?
Why long to obliterate?
You salivate at the mention of hate!
You demand and obligate people to hate!
You scream and gyrate with hate!
You idolize the ingrate!
You teach your kids to partake in hate!
You think love is irate!
You believe the lie that you don't hate!
You are what's wrong in this holy debate!
Embracing and encouraging love,
In exchange for all that hate,
Or has hate sealed your fate?!
Like Pilate, Nero, and Hitler you adulate!
I implore you, in love, to capitulate.
God wins the debate
of love vs. hate.
Checkmate!

Cold Shoulder

A badge and a gun,
I have already won
Especially if you run.
I was created to police,
Mainly for the golden fleece,
And with the protection of legalese
Together with my gun and badge, I kill peace.
Fear, drugs, sex, and hate,
These are what we perpetuate
While we wonder will all this abate.
Protect and serve is used to exonerate.
Are we any different from the Roman soldier?
Is our democracy in foreclosure?
Was it all an illusion of grandeur?
Have we given God the cold shoulder?

Fake, Fake, Fake

Fake news
    Fake posts
        Fake people behind both

Fake News

Fake news,
what an oxymoron while singing the blues.
With your only clues,
being those same claimed
fake news!
Reveling in the darkness of chaos
and being at a loss
for ambiguity
you whine in perpetuity
to a rallying cry
to undermine
a profound crime
to deceive the young mind
too young to know
that fake news
is just a ploy
as old as dirt.
A masterful lie
told by the father of lies
to an acceptable mind,
both blind
and unkind.
Lost in the temptations of this world
while never being as bold
in seeking the truth,
only desiring the poisonous uncouth.

Fall Up

One equals too
and my foot is two big for my shoe;
Two is greater than ate,
and ate is less than sicks
but after the junk I eight,
I think I'm going to be six.
A lying world emerges n sees
where nothing makes scents
but cents, the people lost yes turd day.
Never paying at ten Sean
Peep Al change the rules
to a common man date for their lies.
Making up shh hit
like a pass thyme.
Ignoring Avia's warning,
two smart for hour own good.
While we r bee n dumbed down.
Stand up twoetal,
less we fall up.

Forty-Five

Why is it so hard for you to see
      that this President has taken a knee
      on the throat of this country?
Or is it really you and me?!
Read on to see.
He doesn't care about you and me,
      he only cares about his electability.
Is this really what we think of being free?
His ego is bigger than the Presidency.
If we are not careful or live in mediocrity,
      we are driving this country into tyranny.
You elected the worst of many
      many more men with greater empathy
      which could have done better than he
      and all from the same political party.
It is the Senate anyway
      that has given him every victory,
      and this would have happened with any
      of the other men that ran from that party.
The lie he convinced you to believe in unity,
      is that he really cares about this country.
When truth be told, he likes to star on TV.
In matters of state, he is a dancing monkey,
      dancing to the tune of enmity.
My country tis of thee,
      sweet land of liberty
      to you I make this plea,
      we cannot afford his majesty!

He tears us apart with his lying tapestry,
> wanting only misery
> for a huge portion of our citizenry.

Never in my life could I predict this imagery
> of my country
> rushing to the stage for the victory
> of bigotry.

He is causing all this despair daily
> only thinking and banking on a victory
> so he can erode the last of our dignity,
> all in the name of saving humanity.

A showman, at best, and his idolatry
> for whatever plays best on TV
> and for his candidacy.

He hears your fear of ingenuity
> and your cries of hypocrisy
> tallying these up to democracy

and claiming a race war on hospitality.
Now we don't trust anybody.
Our love empty
> of any real empathy
> of those with a different story
> or memory.

Repeating history
> of great nations falling into heresy
> when our leaders deceive sanctity
> by the hypocrisy
> that a newborn and religion is our vitality
> while stoking the evil flames of enmity
> all the while erasing our human dignity
> and promoting violence on his enemy.

Screams rise to elect the other party,
> only bringing another type of instability
> which is a doctrine of kill the baby
> while proclaiming it a health necessity

        and claim they uphold human dignity
        all in the name of religious impunity!
What people don't get is the parity
        of a democracy
        striving for equality
        without instability
        but in unity.
It's our fault that leaders lack creativity
        and profess an open hostility
        because we hold the power over stability
        but we have deferred to eligibility
        and refused tranquility
        as an emotional plea
        and to glee
        over the power we can direct over thee.
So simple, do you see?
This President is not our enemy
        he is what is wrong with you and me!
He only represents our worse quality,
        our fear of each other and sustainability.
He gives us permission to forgo formality
        which we deplore in our new reality.
We are the enemy
        you and me
        we the people are rebuking commonality
        for the lust of insatiable insanity.
No, it is not the President's majesty
        it is our boredom with sensibility
        and frustration with heredity
        that establishes an impaired serenity
        that lacks popularity
        while all we crave
        is popularity!

Forsaking all serenity
      for the greatest trophy
      the all-important me!
What is needed from you and me
      is a will to explore humility
      and embrace civility.

God's Xanadu

Hey ho,
where did all the food go?
This is a good time to fast,
or that TP you just bought will not last!
There is only one reason you fear,
and it has nothing to do with what you hear.
What has you scared,
is that your morals are impaired.
It's not too late
to get rid of all that hate.
All you must do
is walk away from the old you,
and turn anew to God's Xanadu.

Hail to the Mischievous

Coochi coochi coo
You lost foo
More people didn't want you
And those that do
Jim Jones had a following too
Hard to understand why
We fall for the satan lie
As more people die
We drink the punch and sigh
Looking people in the eye
We continue to spread the lie
All in good time
Just don't drink the poisoned wine
The belief that all is fine
That the cure is on the vine
There's still plenty of time
While all our leader can do is whine
Boohoo and crying its mine
All mine
We look to the future in the dark
We listen to each other bark
No love for our Patriarch
We try to install a Monarch
Who's only hallmark
The lie, loving only his trademark

We repeat the cycle of hate
We relinquish our fate
While fake power becomes irate
It can still initiate
A terrible and grotesque debate
The people's power we should negate
Out of hate
And set a destructive mandate
Let us open the evil floodgate
Woe to us
Hailing the mischievous!

Historic Virus and a Political Mess

Political parties are just a friction clutch.
You talk too much,
and why you in such a rush
to tell everyone to hush?
Why you drinking all that political punch?
Is it because they say so much
about what causes you strife and such?
Or because you are out of touch?
Maybe it's just a political crutch?

Either or, you do keep score.
This just tells me you want more.
No matter the party it has become your core
and just as senseless as idle folklore.
Too interested in the abject abhor!
Get a grip, all you do is deplore
and ignore.

Try to implore a new scheme,
try to work as a team.
To each his own is just obscene,
and no one wants the lazy extreme.

So, there is an opportunity
for unity
if we start with dismissing incredulity.
Start the conversation with impunity.

What do we have to lose?
Except maybe that bruise
to an egotistical pride.
Don't try to hide
and chide
behind reports that coincide
with your evil snide.

Be better than this
and dismiss
your desire to be remiss!

Look at what is happening this Easter!
It is kicking us in our collective keester.

We should band together in love,
as instructed from above.

The way we steer out of this mess,
is playing nice with lovingly kindness!

I Will Be Just Fine

My eyes are not as young as before,
My heart is not as cold
But my spirit is bubblier than ever!
Or at least that is what I was just told
yesterday and I'm pushing fifty-four.
When I was just a tot
Like any little boy, I played outdoors a lot.
Somewhere between here and there
I found despair,
or it found me, I can't really tell.
It just snuck up out of nowhere.
So, I turned back inside to hide from me,
To bury what I found
Deep in the corner of my soul.
An obnoxious asshole.
Pardon my French,
But that's what I found in that trench.
A trench full of broken hope
With little pieces everywhere
And none of them fit my mold.
Depression gained its hold
And for thirty-five years I was all alone.
Living but not living
Laughing but not laughing
Loving but not loving at all.
Walking slowly backwards
Away from it all
And screaming, what is wrong with me?
But not loud enough for anyone to hear.

I only whispered it into my own ear
Steering clear of myself,
While I cried myself to sleep.
I'm wide awake
While I hide,
I take a deep breath to clear my mind.
I work at clearing the web of lies
I weaved inside my heart,
With the help of the things
that have influenced my thoughts.
Help me!
I scream into the headwind of time.
Time to take control of my life,
Past the time to pick hope off the vine
And smile from time to time.
Because in the end,
I will be just fine!
I choose to stop dining
on the whining all the time,
And get back into the game of a lifetime.

I Vote My Faith

For all of you that have the audacity and pride to step into the role of God, let me be clear, stop the fear mongering and hate in this political debate. You cannot take away my faith just because you intimidate and manipulate. My faith is mine to keep because God blessed me with it not because you say I can share in it. My heart belongs to God and I call on His Spirit as Christ instructed me to do. This is where truth comes from, not you telling me what to do. There, I said it! Let it sink in and get off your righteous mantel of screaming at me of what you think I should do. With your false debates of pretentious witness clouding your forgiveness and exchanging it with spiritual fitness. Like you know the difference when truth screams to your heart that there is something terribly wrong. With everyone against each other how can we ever get anything done? You would think this pandemic would bring us together or that senseless killing of any kind would be denounced as unkind but rewind the tape on this debate on which life matters to the master planner. We have all played a role in this matter and we become entangled in our own ignorant chatter. Given to us in a whisper by the master instigator. The one that lost everything in this affair of claiming that God is unfair. His pride, like ours, condemned him to hell. Pray your fate will not end the same because you follow the insane and profane your faith as something that can be bought and sold with an I told you so.

In a Pinch? Stop Dancing with That Winch

Be careful of that holy glare
As we play truth or dare
The day is coming
For that second coming
A giggle here and a wiggle there
We are left to our own despair
For we turned from that holy stare
What do we look for in a King
Something rotting
To be obedient to a fault
You are never too damn smart
This can only bring you joy
None of this wanting to destroy
Just bask in His holy glare
And be mesmerized by His stare
It is only fair
That He should strip us bare
  Of that awful sin
  We beaconed to come in
Forgive me and give me strength
To never again dance with that winch
Turning entangling tightening
Oh I definitely mean winch
In a pinch you are in
That spell of evil sin
Break the spell and start living again without the sin

Life

Hurt, anger, and despair everywhere!
All the while we are getting nowhere.
Complaining and wining about our hair
while people starve and die, but we don't care;
we would rather compare our prayer.
Lies and deceit is our new retreat
while the theme for this circus show is our conceit.
The big attraction is this ill faction
dealing in a greedy transaction
to accommodate those few with the power
to empower their own.
They huddle and muddle
in their racist and bigoted pony show,
while the rest of us are thrown into the freak show.
Not knowing where to go.
Time and time again have we seen this play out,
but now we have this killer milling about
just waiting for that life we throw away
because we say it is better this way.
Frankly, an idiot cannot dismay
as much as the clever man can lead you astray,
but we praise the shrewdness of the wolf in sheep's clothing
while molding our children in the same way.
Letting them get away with betrayal and a foray into lustful play
while tempting fate in a scary way,
but laughing all the way.
Well, for a writer, I don't know what else to write.
I have written how Love can save us from this fuss.
I've written how in God we can trust.

In these poems I have extolled the beauty of virtue.
As your brother I do not think twice
about pointing out the vice
that kept me from being nice.
I share my sinful nature
because we are all in the same pasture
with the same wolves trying to devour us.
I became tired of dancing like a monkey
at the circus masters every request!
I decided to engage in this spiritual war of chess.
My God told me He would bless my every move
and if I listened and obeyed, I would most definitely improve.
One contemplative move,
and be prepared in prayer
for evils counter move.
Intently and purposely, we watch closely
because if we let up in our prayer life
we easily can fall into strife
and we are back where we started
Scared, lost, and hating our life.

People Go Crazy

Swine flu, SARS, Ebola, MERS, and Covid-19 walk into a bar . . .
NO! This sh*t ain't funny.
You need to talk about something more than the Easter bunny.
Hey honey, you pick up that toilet paper from the store?
I want some more,
and just like that,
Sh*t ain't funny no more!
I came back with a broken toe, she yelled back.
It is like addicts buying up the crack.
That's why, my sweet darling says, I had to kick that ho* in her back.
So, before you venture out
Do not pout
It might be you
They put out
Go on, throw them Lboes
So the story can go
She fought hard,
for that last toilet-paper roll!

Ramblings of one Sinner to Another

Hypocrites can pray eloquently; they can sing praises with angelic voices while their coffers and cupboards are full, but God only hears the wailing of the poor and hungry as sweet melody of suffering and humility. Thank you to the rich and greedy because God listens and rewards their victims. Don't let the devil convince pious wannabes that fear, and greed will set you free while you pick up Jesus' body like a McDonald's happy meal or calling it a wafer symbol with Kool-Aid. You call it a bloody symbol and then go back to your sinful ways, hating your brother and his mother. Woe to the others that never partake of the body and blood as Jesus did with His disciples that night He was betrayed. With all your deceit and hypocrisy adopted from the father of lies to convince you that God will not provide for the future of His own church, what pride has gotten hold of you to think a golden calf is what is required for healing and mercy? What has fooled you so to believe that words exceed deeds or that deeds surpass the plea of justice? What is most important is what you find under your precious jewels and robes and abodes adorned with shame, fame, and the same. Where has the love gone, and why is mercy stolen by men, women, boys and girls full of pride? Is it because we honor God with malfeasance and never shout out against the obvious pestilence of snide worship because we always go back to our old ways? Never embracing love as much as we do hate. Never showering mercy at least equally with our duplicity. We hang with Jesus like a grandma but party with satan like a rock star and fail to distinguish the two. It is no wonder God seems not to hear because His church is too busy with its evil lurching my dear. He sent His Son with this message 2000 years ago: love God and neighbor and how is that going?! Just look around at the church on every other corner and every type of flavor while His real church puts their head in the sand, with so much favor and resources they burrow into the safety of a corporate like snake leaving the most vulnerable uninvited, hungry and dejected to fend on mere crumbs while asking them to sacrifice more, like their first born never to drink from that golden chalice behind the protective glass inside a vault.

Priceless is that arrogance, priceless is that pride, priceless is that do or die of the most evil lie out of the lips of our brother. . .just hang in there, we will one day recover. There is one church that can change the world but all it does is snore and acts like a wh*** to the evil of this forlorn world of hypocritical antipathy.

Sin and Guns

That resounding sound is not the sound of peace,
it is the sound of gunfire gone wild.
We love our violent ease,
while our argument is that of a child.
We say this is hard to watch,
but do nothing about what hurts us.
We don't even dare a patch,
we prefer to remain oblivious.
Did we ever really love each other,
the way we love our guns?
Have we always been about the druthers?
Always looking for puns.
What happens to Heaven on earth?
I guess we just forgot.
I guess no one has any worth.
Today, it seems, there is only rot.
From the inside out,
and the outside in
we choose to pout,
but it is our sin,
that we should be talking about.

Slam on the Brakes

A one-man circus show
boasting how he loves us so
letting us die because he won't eat crow.
A one manpower trip
opening his mouth and lies escape his lips.
A one man play on pride
while ignorance follows him in stride.
A one-man mockery of our democracy
while he openly pushes for aristocracy.
A one-man comedy hour
given tribute to himself and his power.
A one-man novela
bragging that he's the smartest fella.
A one-man train wreck,
while only the sane ask, What the heck?!
A one-man tornado
as he tries to restore Jim Crow.
A one-man nightmare
for a country going nowhere, beware!
A one-man trapeze act
selling lies as fact.
A one-man scape goat
for all those who desire pride to gloat.
One man is all it takes
and now it is time to slam on the brakes!

Solitude with Attitude

A Solitude
With an Attitude
Of Gratitude
But Protruding
So crudely
And Ensnaring
While emanating
The cruelty
Of greed
Hypocritically
Fascinating
Enshrined
In particulates
Of lies and deceit
Protagonist
Love
Arrives
Unceremoniously
Cleansing
Ceremoniously peaceful
Overcasting
The destruction
Caused by hate

Start Your Life Anew

Relinquish your zeal for the unreal; those half-truths and lies. Your glory relies on the truth, your couth, and the Lord of the Sabbath. When you advise your brother to believe your druthers, you promote your own demise, my brother. The devil laughs as his lies are promoted, while you stumble into a spiritual gaffe one right after another. Open your eyes to the devil's lies which can fly in a tweet, but you need to submit to the truth of the Paraclete to fully understand this crime. This evil can also suggest that a human right to kill is a bill for equal rights. When you divide and conquer, I do wonder, is it for your own glory you ponder such deceit while you also ask for a receipt? While you hammer that stake into His flesh do you realize you forsake your crown of glory for a partisan story of power and fame? What a shame! Hypnotized and rationalized to think you are a winner while all you become is just another sinner doomed to the fall. You still have time to shine like new, it is only a matter of when to throw down that hammer and start your life anew!

The Evil Game

Come and take me away from this dark place where only the lonely play, repeatedly.

The game never ends and never begins, it is just an endless race to a place that doesn't exist.

There is no finish line, there is only that perpetual race to get to no place fast without consideration to those who need my help around me and all around me.

I see them reaching out, their hearts in hand, but I walk right past them in a hurry

with no time to consider their pain, much less the heart they carry in their hand.

How it must hurt to carry your heart in your hand as the cold envelopes around it.

There is no sense of time, while clocks and watches tell of a time gone by but tells nothing of the

time to come.

                Can I get an amen?

                No, you may not!

There is no time for a fairytale of a King without land in this broken-down sham!

Once all that was needed was to tell a chosen people that "I Am" said so but now it is a different time

with only a cold and callous, "Because I said so."

Everything has been mocked and frocked with lies and deceit only so that it satisfies a greedy

conceit.

Woe to me in this ill retreat, woe to you too for believing my lie as I looked right into your eye.

As I stared and waited for you to respond with the answer I expect in response.

The only acceptable, I believe you.

Like a jewel in my crown, I hold my head up high.
You believe my lie!
And we start this evil game all over again,
with no end or beginning, just one endless circle of evil's applause,
                                            and the laughs he laughs
                                                            as he laughs his ass off.

Tragic and Lost

I'm wide awake and hearing the fake,
trying to figure out how this happened,
our culture collapsing,
heading to somewhere we can't go.
To a place of hate,
a statement to the fate of mankind.
Things come to mind when I look behind
to a place I thought we left behind the first time,
the second time, third time is the charm, a fourth?
When do we stop pressing repeat?
Bittersweet, but all can agree
religion in trickles, and politics being fickle.
We got ourselves a pickle folks!
Be bold you blokes,
women don't stoke the bloat of these
you give birth to the defenseless
you keep afloat
the boat of compassion and love.
Truth and lies.
Tragic and lost.
A nation's shame, with not all to blame?
Could I have done more?
Will I speak from one side then the other?
Can I trust in Faith when it tells me the same shame?
And more of the same?
No, because faith has no shame!

Truth Trumpet

A con man with a megaphone
and you are right where you want to be
in this evil environment of
what is in it for me?
He stokes the flames of hate
and you ravishingly devour the bait
buying that lie of making us great.
You silly puppet
There was already a truth trumpet
but his posse likens you to Him
with an obnoxious and vile comparison.
How can you stand your reflection?
In making such a wild and sick inflection?
The shame is this demon's claim
while winning your unvarnished fame.
He plays this hideous game
of deceit and conceit
while his tribe
is all about the whine
of the woe is me
and pass the fine wine of division
and malnutrition of a people
starving to be free.
Never have we chosen to be so naive
except before all these libraries
but even so,
there was always the Word
serving as our guide
to love's tributary

connecting us to God's accord
which warned of this dark hour.
We stare and listen like star struck children
eager to please and applaud the master's sick deeds
while he fools you to believe
that he is in it to protect us
from the harm he has caused us
in his own pursuit, of what is in it for me.
What is the difference in killing a life from killing a soul?
Did you not read the same Word?
Do not wait around for an I told you so.
By then it will be too late
to escape all his hate
and the ill fate that comes home
to roam in cold hearts
beckoning division with shrewd attrition
and calling him a heavenly intervention.
The best you can do is fast and pray,
the Holy Spirit will lead your way
because God sent the Holy Spirit to stay
teaching, enlightening and keeping you from being led astray.
All you must do is open your heart to love and hope
and then ask yourself
is he really dope?
Or the devil's scheme to make me someone's dope on a rope?

Weak

How lame are we when we are meant for greatness,
the thought of people raped for a cleansing of the population
repels no one and nobody
but a run on the store to buy more guns
invokes a euphoria of a false security
while some are too eager to sell them
because they believe they are valiant
and honorable.

How wrong is wrong?

Leaders that think of others as a number
trickles down to my brother, sister, mother, and father.
What is one more number when we have so many?
We pamper and protect our pets,
We feed them, clothe them, and keep them safe.
We punish those who would violate them, hurt them.
While those with two arms, two legs, a heart ,and a soul
We revile the very thought they exist,
Disturbing my interests.

How cruel is cruel?

We penetrate our children,
We excite over failure,
We demure our hate,
We blender the unborn,
We trophy sex
We cheer on the bully

How can anyone love us?

W-inless bribes,
E-mpty powers,
A-ngry anger,
K-nowledgeable ignorance.

Backward and forward,
up and down,
side to side,
we do not know what we are doing.
Oh, but we do!
We really, really know what we do.

Well, Well

Well, well what do you know?
Trolling around, but not wanting
to grow
or are you the type who cheapens his own
by thinking that you own your own
throne?
You earn your crown
by calling out the brown, the different and the broke down.
What people are this?
Asking JESUS to loan them His crown?
Have not the same type always let you down
because they wear a permanent frown?
They claim to know Jesus but all the while,
they are nothing more than a performing clown.

What Choice in Fallen World

I railed against our leader the other day
don't start cheering that I think your way!
While you accept that there is no God
in all your indulgent and sinful ways.
You say you are for love and peace
while you laugh at us that fall to our knees to pray.
Can you not see that malice coming from all your pride?
While you sit in judgement's snide.
Saying you pray for our leader
and to me it could not be any clearer
that you hand over the cleaver
to the necks of babies not yet delivered.
What choice is your choice?
Nothing better, you both hate the other.
What I desire is what no one offers
a loving reality that does not fill greed's coffers!
We deserve leaders thinking of how to unite our country
in love and saving us from a great big fall.
I see no such leader on either side,
I only see that both sides are full of pride.
I know what side I am on
and it is the one no one can own!
The only side that has no pride.
The one who is slow to chide.
The one that will not hide.
The God of love, who loves everyone,
His only begotten Son
and the Holy Spirit.
This is the side that won!

The only side that will give you a crown.
So, if there was any doubt
or you knew what I was all about
you missed all my other poems,
messages and omens.
Stop with the hate
and learn the real debate.
Stop with your judgements
this is far from your job
and not even one of our sacraments!
Take off your righteous vestments
and turn to humility, now this is a good investment
and peel away all that resentment.
We all sin, we are all unworthy
but we are not in Kansas anymore Dorothy
there is only one way to be worthy.
Empty yourself of self
and fill yourself
with faith, love, charity
and be just for perfect clarity!
So, rise above the hate and lies on both sides
and realize,
there is only one side that counts.
We the people need to hold our leaders to account.
Even if your side wins
remember all people have sins
and we must call out those sins
just as enthusiastically as we praise their wins.
Otherwise, we all lose, and no one wins
because we keep embracing our sin.

Will We Burn?

an insult for an insult
an evil exchanged for evil
hate thrown at hate
a lie to answer a lie
fear to stir up fear
a jeer to combat a sneer
a callous action for a callous action
cruelty vs cruelty
hopeless peddling hopelessness
gluttony feeding greed
lust in lust for lust
pride glorifying pride
scorn to scorn
evil denied
will we ever learn
before we burn

Wrong Choices

I stagger and fall from high to tall
endless nights call
while I build a wall
igniting a lonely recall
and an evil brawl
which makes me crawl
while the devil throws a masked ball
and I fake appall
trying to forestall
while satan screams, winner takes all
he hands me a death shawl
I feel dumb and small
I stall
I wrawl
but evils befall
to a loud catcall
hooray for your fall
gnashing of teeth and all
an evil windfall
a heavenly blackball
guilty of my own downfall
free will and all
and I chose a shortfall
I should have chosen a prayer shawl
there is no next time, y'all

Yesterday, Today, and Tomorrow I lie

I run afoul my faith
I say God chose yesterday
but the devil stole today,
tomorrow, I suppose, a malignant wraith!
I do not see my hypocrisy
because I have lived in a lie,
today I hear, see and speak only to deny.
Tomorrow, I suppose, a higher frequency!
I am my own expert
for I found a blowhorn's mendaciousness
and I made it my own righteousness.
Tomorrow, I suppose, a raucous disport!
I see no wrong because my lie is true
I accepted it long before yesterday,
walking proudly in a charlatan's foray.
Tomorrow, I suppose, no breakthrough!
I own the lie
I bought the swindle
to peddle and rekindle.
Tomorrow, I suppose, another lie!

Epilogue

All my life I can remember being an independent thinker and believing that God gave me the free will to do just that, decide my own fate.

My best friend describes me as a walking contradiction and I would have to agree. I experience life as a five-dimensional game of chess with five active players. Any player can make a move and does not have to wait for you to make a countermove. In my version of the game the five players are God the Father, God the Son, God the Holy Spirit, the satan, and I. My five-dimension game board consists of the spiritual, the material, the emotional, providence, and compulsion.

Questions I ask myself to keep sharp in order to succeed in the five-dimensional game of life: Is there a place in my heart for truth even when it bruises my pride? Is there enough love in me to console my anger? Is my courage fierce enough to overcome my fear? Is my perseverance sustainable when my passions want to run wild? Is my self-control strong enough to endure repeated enticement from my vanity? Is my empathy such as to quell my lust? Is my charity greater than my gluttony? Am I able to be truthful to myself about myself when I'm all alone? What do I believe and why do I believe it?

The poems that you just experienced are an insight to how God answered my questions or prayers. Praying is the most beautiful thing you can do to show God how much you love Him and your neighbor. He may not give you poems, but He will give you what you need. I promise because

Jesus promised, God promises, and the Holy Spirit fulfills the promise. You simply must ask, knock or seek Him in love.

True to my nature, I am writing a tale based on true events about the forces within each one of us that prompts and entices us, influencing our choices in this life while having profound consequences on our journey. I invite you to come along with me on this journey. It all starts in Asherton, TX at a fiesta at the small plazita when my dad (below on the left, my great grandfather is on his right) meets my mother and it was love at first site. Stay tuned . . . I have a Love story to tell.

www.ingramcontent.com/pod-product-compliance
Lightning Source LLC
Chambersburg PA
CBHW071424150426
43191CB00008B/1035